SY 0118912 3

GH01033038

ST. MARY'S UNIVERSITY CC
LIBRARY
A COLLEGE OF THE QUEENS UNIVERSITY OF BELFAST

Tel. 028 90327678
Web site www.stmarys-belfast.ac.uk
email: library@stmarys-belfast.ac.uk

Fines will be charged for overdue and recalled books not returned by
stated date.

AN   N

Date Due	Date Due	Date Due
1- 3 NOV 2010		
2 2 NOV 2010		
2 5 APR 2012		
1 9 NOV 2012		
1 3 NOV 2014		
- 5 FEB 2016		
- 6 JUN 2016		
2 2 FEB 2018		

Price $2.00 Postpaid

PUBLISHED BY THE AUTHOR

22 East 17th Street   :   .   :   New York City

COPYRIGHT, 1924, BY HERMON F. BELL

Printed in the United States of America

PETER G. BOYLE, BOOK MANUFACTURER, NEW YORK

CONTENTS

CHAPTER 1

This little book does not attempt an ordered or systematic presentation of theology. It is the writer's belief that such a work rightly conceived and well carried out is the greatest need of the world today. There has been great progress in all sciences but theology. In fact it may be said that new sciences have been established which have greatly extended the knowledge available to us all. There is, however, a singular lack of progress in theology and practically no publication of worth while books upon the subject.

But even more striking than this lack of theological publications is the common feeling, even among many leaders in organized religious work, that the scarcity of books on theological subjects is a blessing rather than otherwise. Why do these conditions exist?

This little book the writer has chosen to call an introduction to theology because it attempts to deal with such questions as the following:

Is theology a science or is a science of theology possible?

Is there any benefit, practical or otherwise, to be derived from study of theology, or will such study simply lead to controversy with discord and disagreement as the only result?

Assuming that theology is both possible and desirable, by what basic methods and on what principles or foundation must it be constructed or developed?

What of Christian theology as represented on the one hand by the historic creeds and confessions, or on the other by so-called liberal Christians? What are the fundamentals of these two types of so-called Christian theology and what judgment is to be passed upon them today?

Is it possible to develop and state in clear, unequivocal, understandable language, a theology which a critical but a sincere man can, nay must, believe in, and if so what are the main outlines of such a theology?

In this introductory chapter a few words seem to be in order upon two subjects, the qualifications of the writer for the work undertaken and the purpose and spirit of the book.

The writer is reluctant to discuss the former question. In the larger sense either his qualifications or lack of them will be judged by the book itself. Any testimony regarding himself is not needed nor required, nor will, nor should, it be accepted except as substantiated by what he writes in the chapters following. However, because in all the professions there is a disposition, perhaps for the most part justified, to consider as of little or no account the opinions or writings upon professional subjects of those not belonging to that profession, and because the writer is not an ordained clergyman, he makes a very brief statement with respect to the training and experience which justify his writing upon the subjects included in this book.

The writer was born, as it were, into the orthodox Congregational Church of which he became a member as the most natural course at the age of eleven. He graduated from Amherst College in 1901. It was there that he received the deepest religious impressions of his life, and by Professor C. E. Garman, of blessed memory, was introduced to thought and study of theological, philosophical, and religious problems. He attended Massachusetts Institute of Technology for a year of specialized study, but found the impressions made by Professor Garman so strong as to render it impossible for him then to study any other subject than theology. He accordingly spent three years at Yale Divinity School, graduating in 1905 and being licensed to preach by the New Haven Association of Congregational Ministers. Although licensure was obtained, not without difficulty, however, on the basis of or perhaps rather in spite of practically the same theology still held and outlined in this book, it will not be difficult for the reader to understand why it was necessary to adopt as a means of livelihood a profession other than the ministry. For twenty years the writer has studied and pondered over these problems.

The theology outlined in this book was arrived at in practically its present form before graduation from Yale Divinity School in 1905. The writer cannot, however, truthfully give so much thanks as he would wish to that school, as nearly all that he learned there seems to him to have been negative. It was, however, worth while to learn that many things formerly believed were not so. It is also with grateful recollection that he remembers friendships there formed and the extremely valuable opportunities afforded of attendance at graduate philosophical courses in the University, and perhaps most of all for the Seminary library where one could read and read and read.

George Eliot wrote, "Most of us who turn to any subject with love remember some morning or evening hour when we got on a high stool to reach down an untried volume, or sat with parted lips listening to a new talker, or for very lack of books began to listen to the voices within, as the first traceable beginning of our·love."

The writer's love for and belief in theology dates from his entrance into the class of Professor Garman at Amherst in the year 1900. At the death of Professor Garman in 1907, Dr. Lyman Abbott wrote in *The Outlook* concerning him the following words,—"He guided the thinking of his students towards what he believed to be sound conclusions. . . . Some of them did not reach his conclusions; more of them forgot the conclusions which they did reach; but practically all of them were inspired by the spirit of free inquiry, and with the conviction that free inquiry conducted with reverence for the truth can be trusted eventually to reach trustworthy conclusions. The affectionate respect with which the graduates from his class room look back upon him can be compared only so that with which Thomas Arnold has been regarded by·the graduates of Rugby." The following was from the pen of Professor William James of Harvard. in *The Nation* of August 9, 1906, concerning Professor Garman. "He . . . devoted all his energies to being an inspiring teacher; and his "publishing" has been only of pamphlets for the use of his successive classes. The results have been extraordinary in their effect, not only on the intellect. but on the character of those who have come under his influence."

At the very beginning of this book the writer wishes to acknowledge his overwhelming debt to Professor Garman. In no sense, however, should the theology or the conclusions herein stated be ascribed to Professor Garman. The writer asks the reader to give such credit if he finds anything worth while but whatever of error is found let it be attributed to the writer himself. He knows that he has arrived at many conclusions which are his own, and which, if found faulty, are not to be ascribed to anyone else. While the writer believes his conclusions are logical, he does not claim that they are those of Professor Garman. The latter left only fragmentary writings, published after his death by his widow through Houghton Mifflin Co., under the title, "Letters, Lectures and Addresses of Charles Edward Garman,—A Memorial Volume." Numerous quotations therefrom are used in this book.*

This acknowledgment of indebtedness to Professor Garman is not made for the purpose of hiding behind a great name or of seeking to gain weight for the views herein presented by reference to him or to the college he so faithfully served. The writer imputes these opinions to no school, or to no individual; he speaks for himself alone, and acknowledges that he has drawn conclusions and made applications that he has not heard from anyone. At the same time he makes no claim for originality because he knows in his heart how greatly he is indebted to Professor Garman for his fundamental approach to the entire problem. The sense of this indebtedness has increased rather than diminished with each passing year.

---

* With the permission of the publishers, which is gratefully acknowledged.

PURPOSE AND SPIRIT OF THIS BOOK

Attention has already been called to the fact that recent progress seems to have been made in all sciences except theology. Think of the marvelous progress constantly being made in all other sciences as well as in business organization and management, and then consider the case of theology. Life has been well nigh revolutionized within the memory of men now living. There are new means of communication and what were formerly comforts and luxuries have become necessities. Yet there has been little admitted change in theological and religious teachings, however much men's beliefs may have unconsciously changed, or drifted toward tolerant scepticism or unbelief. When have you heard real unrestricted discussion of fundamental theological and religious questions? No wonder that young men and women coming each year in increasing numbers from colleges and universities find it ever and ever more difficult to synthesize their science and their religion. Either they have to hold religion as a thing apart from science, art, business and even from life itself, or adopt the modern liberal theology which is often in reality another name for religious scepticism and indifference, with emphasis upon morality, without deep religious foundation. It is a great misfortune when science and religion cannot go hand in hand. Science, morals, and religion all suffer from separation or divorce.

"I think it is conceded that one is so far justified in believing in natural law in the spiritual world as to affirm that what holds of gravitation holds of our moral life. As our physical weight depends upon the size of the planet in which we live, as a man who weighs one hundred and fifty pounds on the earth would weigh more than a ton if transported to a body as large as the sun, so it is with our mental weight. It depends upon the size of the world in which we consciously live. The man who takes a superficial view of the great problems of human life, and the great truths of religion, narrows himself as much as he does his world; he becomes frivolous, insincere, cynical, the prey to all sorts of temptation and moral degradation. For this there is no other remedy than a more profound apprehension of the truth. You can make him pharisaical by natural means, but you can make him religious only by the truth."—Garman.

This book is written in the belief that there is truth, and that truth may be arrived at by study, discussion and research, not all at once, but in part at least, and sufficient for our daily need. Any one who deals with figures or attempts to balance accounts cannot fail to be impressed with the fact that errors do not balance, that only when errors have been eliminated can the accountant be satisfied and be assured as to the correctness of his work. Try to conceal them as one will, errors come up to trouble and discomfort; correctness and satisfaction are to be obtained only by meeting and overcoming not by avoiding difficulties. In this book we are not interested in what we may possibly, by hook or by crook, persuade ourselves or others of. There is no desire but for the truth; not what one may, but what one must believe; what when it is presented one cannot help believing. That is the only theology, the only religion worth having; not something to defend or apologize for, but something that constrains us. A false belief is harmful; Carlyle says, "The first of all Gospels is this, that a lie cannot endure forever."

However desirable it is that there be study, discussion, and presentation of works upon theological subjects, it is useless or worse than useless to attempt such until thorough consideration has been given to underlying premises. At the present time theology seems to be in about the position of astronomy before Copernicus. It was useless or well nigh useless to write volume after volume based upon the Ptolemaic conception of the universe. What was needed as an introduction to the subject was presentation of the Copernican theory, then critical study and discussion, and thereafter a new astronomy based upon new and more adequate premises. This is the method of science. The same method needs to be applied to theology today. Are the Bible and Jesus the central themes of all religion, or do we need to realize that the sun around which all revolves is God Himself?

"There are some who affirm that as a true knowledge of the material heavens was a revelation to men of that very earth with which they supposed themselves so familiar, and transformed their ideas of its size, its importance, and its laws, taking all the flatness out of it, and revealing it to us as one of the stars, so a true knowledge of the spiritual firmament would alter our whole estimate of life; would make many things that now seem of undue importance appear trivial, and other things that are now trivial of prime importance; would for the first time reveal the true dignity and grandeur of human nature."—Garman.

Theology was at one time called queen of the sciences. This was before the modern scientific method was much followed. With the rise of modern science it seems as if there had been taken from the sphere of theology one realm after another. Is it not, however, simply another case of a science needing new premises?

Theology rightly conceived and presented appeals most strongly to all men and women. If it does not so appeal, it is because either the science itself is not rightly conceived or apprehended, or is not clearly presented. The reason for the universal appeal of theology is not far to seek. Only some of us are permanently and deeply interested in chemistry, or in biology, or in geology. But every one is deeply concerned with the subject matter of theology, even though unaware of this fact, for as Augustine said, "Thou hast created us unto Thyself, and our heart finds no rest until it rests in Thee;" or, in the words of Jonathan Edwards, "If the great things of religion are rightly understood, they will affect the heart."

There is need, great need at present, for clear and definite denial and refutation of obsolete or erroneous premises and equally clear statement of new premises. Consequently let no one be dismayed by denials. The object and purpose of this *Introduction to Theology* is constructive, not destructive, namely to state a basis for theological knowledge and belief and for religious assurance, and not to destroy faith, hope, or charity. At the same time, in the discussion of no other subject is there greater need for clearness, and above all for sincerity and honesty. Whatever other faults may rightly or wrongly be imputed to the writer, he hopes that he will not be lacking in clearness or be guilty of evasion or avoidance of difficulties. He aims to use language to express and never to conceal thought. How can one hope to reach the truth without courage and open-minded sincerity? A good motto for any theologian is, "Truth and Freedom; Truth coming from whatever direction, Freedom knowing no bounds but those that truth has set." *

The great philosopher Kant could find nothing unqualifiedly good but a good will. The heroes of mankind, such for example as Jesus and Lincoln to name two illustrations only, are honored above all else for their love and good will to all mankind. The first requisite of a theology is that it be conceived and written in the spirit of good will. If good will be present, only those who believe strongly will dare to deny vehemently. The greatest theologians have insisted upon the need for a spirit of good will. This good will is based not upon sentimentality but primarily upon love toward God and love toward men. The two are inseparable. As we love mankind we learn the love of God, while on the other side love of God inspires us with love of all mankind. Upon this point recall the two great commandments of Jesus and also listen to words of Paul, Augustine and Calvin.

"If I speak with the tongues of men and of angels but have not love, I am become sounding brass or a clanging cymbal."—Paul.

"Blessed is he who loves Thee, and his friend in Thee, and his enemy for Thy sake. He alone loses no dear one, to whom all are dear in Him who is never lost."—Augustine.

"The more closely any person is united to us, the greater claim he has to the assistance of our kind offices, for the condition of humanity requires, that

* Julius H. Seelye, President of Amherst College. 1876-1890.

men should perform more acts of kindness to each other, in proportion to the closeness of the bonds by which they are connected, whether of relationship, or acquaintance, or vicinity; and this without any offense to God, by whose providence we are constrained to it, but I assert that the whole human race, without any exception, should be comprehended in the same affection of love, and that in this respect there is no difference between the barbarian and the Grecian, the worthy and the unworthy, the friend and foe; for they are to be considered in God, and not in themselves, and whenever we deviate from this view of the subject, it is no wonder if we fall into many errors. Wherefore if we wish to adhere to the true law of love, our eyes must chiefly be directed, not to man, the prospect of whom would impress us with hatred more frequently than with love, but to God, who commands that our love to him be diffused among all mankind; so that this must always be a fundamental maxim with us, that whatever be the character of a man, yet we ought to love him because we love God."—Calvin.

In the chapters which follow it seems necessary and desirable to discuss thoroughly questions that seem fundamental in the religious beliefs of men and women. Beliefs cherished by many will be denied. Perhaps some new ideas will be presented.

May not the reader and the writer together enter upon these chapters with the prayer of Augustine on their lips and in their hearts. "Have a pity, O Lord God, lest they who pass by trample on the unfledged bird; and send Thine angel, who may restore it to its nest, that it may live until it can fly."

Also let us take to heart the words of a teacher, "Be not afraid to entertain a new idea, for in so doing some have entertained even the truth although unawares." *

And once again the writer bespeaks for himself from any critic and hopes himself to have the spirit which prompted Epictetus to write, "A guide, when he hath found one straying from the way, leads him into the proper road and does not mock him or revile him, and then go away. And do thou show such a man the truth, and thou shalt see that he will follow it. But as long as thou dost not show it, mock him not, but be sensible of thine own incapacity."

---

* Professor Garman.

CHAPTER II

Several questions confront us, among which are the following:

What is the subject matter of theology?

Is theology a science or can the scientific method be followed therein?

Is not theology different and distinct from the sciences in that religion is revealed and theology is confined to exposition of the truths of religion as made known to men by revelation?

Is theology to be confined to Christian theology or used as a term synonymous therewith?

Anyway, what is to be gained by discussion of theological questions? Has not theology separated men, and brought in hatred and strife? For example, will it not be objected that Calvin, in spite of his noble expression of love towards all men grounded in love of God, as quoted in the preceding chapter, could destroy Servetus for differences in theology? Is there not now happily a tendency to discard theology and theological controversies and emphasize fellowship and human kindness, and point out human fallibility and error and seek consequently a middle course of compromise as a means of religious unity?

First of all let us face squarely the fundamental question. Does theology differ in its very nature from the

19

sciences in that the latter are partial and full of errors and half truths, because the result of human study, research and reasoning, while religion is divine in its origin? Is it true that all scientific knowledge is human in origin, while theology is an explanation or statement of divinely revealed religion? Shall we say that, while theology as a human statement or attempt to explain religion may be faulty, religion itself is divinely revealed and is final and absolute?

No one thinks of sharply differentiating (unless for purposes of historical statement or for recording present development or biographies of leading exponents) as between American, English, French, or German, chemistry. Truth to one is truth to all. But when we come to theology and religion, we find a so-called Christian religion, a so-called Mohammedan religion, a so-called Jewish religion and a so-called Buddhist religion, to mention only four among many, to say nothing of subdivisions of these so-called religions. The common belief among adherents of any religion seems to have been that their religion is perfect and absolute, the whole truth, while other religions are of no account or wholly erroneous. With the growth of wider knowledge, and with wider acquaintance and contact with representatives of various religions, and through study of comparative religions, men and women have become less insistent upon belief in the error and evil of other religions than their own. The view has come to be more and more prevalent that other religions than one's own way may be the result of honest efforts and gropings after truth, but that those religions illustrate the futility of man-made religion, and need to be replaced by the one divinely revealed religion, for example, by Christianity.

Let us come right down to the question of whether or not Christianity is a divinely revealed religion, and if so what are its essential principles, and what doctrines must be held in order to be a Christian. What are the essentials and what the non-essentials of Christian theology?

Upon its weekly church calendar, Plymouth Church, Brooklyn, provides a space where a person desiring to unite with that church may sign the following statement of purpose,—"Believing in the principles of Christian truth and that the increase of their influence is the supreme need of modern society, I desire to unite with Plymouth Church."

This statement of purpose it would seem cannot fail to cause the reader to ask what are the principles of Christian truth. In former days churches were explicit in stating what they believed Christian truth to be. Today it almost seems as if sometimes and in some places general terms or indefiniteness were used because of uncertainty. In the case of Plymouth Church, however, the writer does not believe such to be the reason. but that it is just to say that the apparent purpose is to leave the interpretation and answer to each individual. Even if the invitation then is to every one who calls himself a believer in Christian truth, as he sees it, what, let us ask, is the effect of or the need for this qualifying word Christian? How, if at all, do the principles of Christian truth differ from the principles of truth?

It seems to the writer that we are confronted at the

ST. MARY'S UNIVERSITY COLLEGE

A COLLEGE OF THE QUEEN'S UNIVERSITY OF BELFAST

outset of this Introduction to Theology with a question of prime importance, namely, whether theology is a science at all in the sense of other sciences or whether it is simply an exposition of revealed truth known as Christian truth.

Is the Christian religion a divine revelation? If we set about discussing this question in all its aspects we would ask first of all as to the meaning of the words revelation and divine. In this little book the aim is to avoid long or involved discussions as to words and to meet all questions squarely and answer them briefly.

Among the leaders of the Protestant Reformation there appears a very curious combining of two beliefs or ideas,—first, the right of private judgment or the appeal to reason, and secondly, the authority of the Scriptures. To the writer the two seem absolutely opposed and contradictory. Either the appeal is to reason, or it is to authority, but certainly not to both. The reformers seem not to have felt the inconsistency of their double appeal.

The following quotation is from Calvin:

"But since the perfection of blessedness consists in the knowledge of God. He has been pleased not only to deposit in our minds the seed of religion . . . but so to manifest His perfections in the whole structure of the universe, and daily place Himself in our view, that we cannot open our eyes without being compelled to behold Him. . . .

"Herein appears the shameful ingratitude of men, that though they have in their own persons a factory where countless operations of God are carried on, instead of praising Him, they are the more inflated with pride.

. . . Therefore, another and better help must be given to guide us properly to God as our Creator, and He has added the light of His Word in order to make known His salvation.

"Here it seems proper to make some observations on the authority of Scripture. Nothing can be more absurd than the fiction that the power of judging Scripture is in the Church. When the Church gives it the stamp of her authority, she does not thus make it authentic, but shows her reverence for it as the truth of God by her unhesitating assent. Scripture bears, on the face of it, as clear evidence of its truth as black and white do of their color, sweet and bitter of their taste. It is preposterous to attempt, by discussion, to rear up a full faith in Scripture. Those who are inwardly taught by the Holy Spirit acquiesce in it implicitly, for it carries with it its own testimony.

"It is foolish to attempt to prove to infidels that the Scripture is the Word of God. For it cannot be known to be, except by faith."

So also Luther at the Diet of Worms. The following quotation is from Carlyle speaking of Luther at Worms. "Luther did not desert us. His speech, of two hours, distinguished itself by its respectful, wise and honest tone; submissive to whatsoever could lawfully claim submission, not submissive to any more than that. His writings, he said, were partly his own, partly derived from the Word of God. As to what was his own, human infirmity entered into it; unguarded anger, blindness, many things doubtless which it were a blessing for him could he abolish altogether. But as to what stood on sound truth and the Word of God, he would not recant it. How could he?

'Confute me,' he concluded, 'by proofs of Scripture, or else by plain just arguments. I cannot recant otherwise. For it is neither safe nor prudent to do aught against conscience. Here stand I; I can do no other: God assist me!' "

In the case of the reformers it is to be remembered that, resting upon the authority of Scripture as well as upon plain reason and sound argument, they successfully stood against vast earthly power and led in a great advance of freedom. Even Calvin, however, freely stated that the authority of Scripture must be accepted and could not be proven by discussion. "It cannot be known to be (the Word of God), except by faith."

Galileo set forth the following ingenious position which was in effect that, if sound reason or science and Scripture appeared to conflict, the expositor should seek for hidden meanings in the text, which would bring it into accord with science. "Since the Holy Writ is true, and all truth agrees with truth, the truth of Holy Writ cannot be contrary to the truth obtained by reason and experiment. This being true, it is the business of the judicious expositor to find the true meaning of scriptural passages which must accord with the conclusions of observation and experiment, and care must be taken that the work of exposition do not fall into foolish and ignorant hands."

The question of the authority of the Bible cannot be avoided. Candor requires a plain answer. It is in no special sense whatever authoritative. Some parts of it appeal to the reason and heart and are accepted the same as any other writings that so appeal. Just because a statement is contained in the Bible is no reason for its acceptance. The reformers were illogical and in error as respects the authority of the Scriptures.

It is only by the reason that external authority can be judged. The reason cannot accept authority as such but only truth, as it appeals to the reason. Hence religion is not revealed in a manner different in kind or in quality than science or art. Theology is not exposition of a revealed religion but must follow the method of science.

At first this may seem to be a tremendous loss. The reader is asked to defer judgment until the subject is further discussed later in this book.

No attempt has here been made to go into detail as to the degree or kind of authority the Bible possesses, if such it has. Almost any theologian of liberal training or tendency will today, theoretically at least, agree that the Bible is not an infallible authority. Where theological seminaries and churches fail today is in not setting over against the lost belief in an infallible Bible, belief in God as an indwelling spirit, at once the ground and source of all our science and all our life, the one in Whom and through Whom we have the power of reason, of weighing evidence.

"The present is a time that needs this point of view more than any other period. The higher criticism is a serious experience for many who have considered the Bible the only star in nature's sky,—the single light that God has given to direct our steps. Many feel towards the Bible today as the two disciples did towards Christ when on the way to Emmaus. They said: 'We trusted that it had been he which should have redeemed Israel.'

"Whatever be one's own attitude towards the higher criticism, it is impossible not to sympathize with those who have built their whole faith on verbal inspiration. Their first impressions as they take up the polychrome Bible and see the results of the highest scholarship made visible by the different colors are not unlike that of the colored person in the South who, at a somewhat advanced age, had his first experience in riding in the railroad cars. We can easily imagine how it came to pass that he was frightened to death. For years he has heard of the wonderful invention, but, as he has lived far back in the country, it has been all a myth. At length determined to see with his own eyes, he makes his way to the city; he finds the station, and boards the train. While sitting there wondering how it will seem to ride so fast, he notices the train on the other track begin to move in an opposite direction; at first very slowly, and then more swiftly, until it makes him dizzy to look at it. This is followed by an interminable line of freight cars, and, to his infinite surprise, these are followed by a whole procession of high board fences and telegraph poles. And when these have gotten by, terrible to relate, the whole landscape is traveling past him at a furious rate. Can he believe his eyes? Can rocks and mountains move? Surely it is so. There can be but one explanation: it is the very Day of Judgment for is it not written on that day 'The little hills shall skip like lambs, and the mountains like rams at the presence of the Lord, at the presence of the Lord of the whole earth'?

"Modern scholarship gives the lay mind something of a similar shock; and not a few are so frightened that their religious faith expires completely. But could the preacher hold up beside the higher criticism the philosophic view which makes all nature and human history the word of God, and show that revelation is a commentary on those great truths of the moral life which God has written, not on tables of stone, but on the fleshy tables of our hearts, then the congregation would discover that the fundamental truths of religion are unchanged by all the changes that are taking place about us, and that the foundations of God stand sure." *

* From a lecture delivered by Professor C. E. Garman in 1898 before the Yale Divinity School and as Carew Lecture before the Hartford Theological Seminary.

CHAPTER III

In these modern times many theologians are coming forward and saying in effect that, although belief in the infallibility of the Bible is not necessary or in fact in order, yet the Bible will ever retain its unique importance because of its testimony to Christ.

At the end of the last chapter there was quoted a passage which emphasized the need of setting over against the higher criticism of the Bible, "the philosophic view that makes all nature and human history the word of God."

Orthodox theology has taught and still teaches that Jesus of Nazareth is God. Are we to center our religious thought and devotion around Jesus Christ? Do we believe in his deity, or at least in his divinity, whatever may be the distinction or meaning of these terms? This is the subject of the present chapter together with the kindred question of what it is to believe in or accept his divinity.

As a background to so-called liberal Christianity or even to socialized religion which may not insist upon or use the word Christian, and by way of contrast, it may not be out of place to summarize historic orthodox Protestant theology.

One of the writings of Jonathan Edwards published after his decease was entitled "The Work of Redemption." The preface says, "Mr. Edwards had planned a body of

28

divinity, in a new method, and in the form of a history; in which he was first to show, how the most remarkable events, in all ages from the fall to the present time, recorded in sacred and profane history, were adapted to promote the work of redemption; and then to trace, by the light of Scripture prophecy, how the same work should be yet further carried on even to the end of the world. His heart was so much set on executing this plan, that he was considerably averse to accept the presidentship of Princeton college, lest the duties of that office should put it out of his power."

The following quotation is from the early part of that book.

"I would divide the whole space of time into three periods: The

1st. Reaching from the fall of man to the incarnation of Christ;—the

2nd. From Christ's incarnation till his resurrection; or the whole time of Christ's humiliation;—the

3rd. From thence to the end of the world.

It may be some may be ready to think this a very unequal division: And it is so indeed in some respects. It is so, because the second period is so much the greatest: For although it be so much shorter than either of the other, being but between thirty and forty years, whereas both the others contain thousands; yet in this affair that we are now upon, it is more than both the others. I would therefore proceed to show distinctly how the work of redemption is carried on from the fall of man to the end of the world, through each of these periods in their order; which I would do under three propositions; one concerning each period.

I. That from the fall of man till the incarnation of Christ, God was doing those things that were preparatory to Christ's coming, and working out redemption, and were forerunners and earnests of it.

II. That the time from Christ's incarnation, till his resurrection, was spent in procuring and purchasing redemption.

III. That the space of time from the resurrection of Christ to the end of the world, is all taken up in bringing about or accomplishing the great effect or success of that purchase."

While even today theology such as stated in the foregoing outline is held by some, it seems to students of science, and to many others also, as archaic as Ptolemaic astronomy is. It centers around the work of Christ, as Ptolemaic astronomy did about a single planet, the earth. Men's outlook upon the world and history has been so greatly widened as to make untenable certain of the premises fundamental in the orthodox theology. And yet criticism of that theology should ever remember that it probably did synthesize the science and history of that time. Are we to abandon and discard theology and the philosophy of history or should we seek a wider synthesis, such as shall avail itself of today's science and history?

For the most part today it seems as if the so-called more liberal or advanced thinkers, those who have accepted the results of science and the higher criticism, are emphatic in stating that theology has in the past been harmful, and to put it most mildly has outlived its usefulness.

Over against the orthodox position of the past let us place a few modern liberal positions, which differ in emphasis and outlook but as a rule emphasize social service rather than individual regeneration, and hold up as the ideal, restoration of the simple religion of Jesus and fellowship with Christ by accepting and following his spirit of service. It is not the writer's intention to comment at length upon these positions in this chapter. There is somewhat of merit in them, but when all is said they do not, in the writer's opinion, fully meet the present need. Three quotations are here given as illustrative of present day tendencies.

Are we to make our religion simply love of Jesus and acceptance of his spirit of service? Is there no direct relation of each individual to God Himself which is determinative and fundamental? Is all religion and theology to be merged in social service, or do we still need philosophy and theology and constant study of the ground and basis of individual and social duties, privileges, and relationships? It is often difficult to judge as to what is cause and what is effect, whether for example or to what extent one's theology determines one's social outlook and ideas or to the reverse. The writer believes it to be within the province of theology to clarify political and social questions, or rather to supply the basic beliefs and governing principles.

But now for statements of modern liberal or even radical positions. The quotations that follow have been chosen because it is believed that they state clearly and strongly their respective positions.

Rev. John Haynes Holmes of the Community Church of New York in 1922 published a book entitled "New Churches for Old." The following quotations are taken from the concluding chapter.

"Christianity, as it first appeared in Palestine and was

carried by Paul to the Gentiles, is the greatest movement
for human emancipation that history has known . . .
The substance of this primitive Christianity was the moral
passion and hope of Israel; in all that properly belonged
to its composition, it was Jewish to the core. Its quick-
ening spirit was the personality of Jesus of Nazareth, the
last of the prophets and himself the supreme religious
genius of all time. Its gospel was the 'good news' of a
righteous society established on earth as a brotherhood
ordered by the law of love to the end of peace—a gospel
of simple human relationships delivered of the superstition, formalism and racial exclusiveness of later Judaism."

"The great gift which Protestantism conferred upon
mankind was emancipation from ecclesiastical tyranny
. . . Central to the life of this amazing period, was the
discovery of the individual soul as set over against institutions of every kind whatsoever. It was democracy at
work in its first great endeavor after freedom and the
rights of man."

"But Protestantism, if it freed mankind from one corruption, brought along another of its own. In place of
ecclesiasticism it put not religion but theology; for the
tyranny of the church and its officers, it substituted the
equal tyranny of the creed and its dogmas."

"For all of the last four hundred years, religion in
Protestant Christendom has meant acceptance of some
particular type of theological belief. . . . Until comparatively recent times no acceptance of the Christian gospel
was possible without simultaneous acceptance of the story
of the Jews as set down in the Old Testament, the crea-
tionist theory of the origin of life, the Davidic author-
ship of the Psalms, the miracles of Jesus, the resurrec-

tion of the dead (at least in the case of the Nazarene),
and a philosophy of history based on the central idea of
the Atonement; and even today, in most Protestant
churches, these ideas are still used as the familiar test of
spirituality. They are at least as generally characteristic
of thought inside the churches as their rejection is characteristic of thought outside the churches."

"It is this situation which calls at this moment for a
new reformation, as effective in its attack on Prostestant-
ism as the Reformation of Luther and Calvin was effective in its attack on Catholicism. It is not enough to correct the errors of orthodox theology on the basis of the
latest information imparted by modern scientific studies.
This is what the liberals have been all too content to do,
on the supposition, apparently, that all will be well if
the Darwinian theory of origins is substituted for the
Mosaic. and the conclusions of the higher criticism of the
Bible accepted without reservations! What is needed is
something much more fundamental and therefore revolutionary. We must get rid not only of theological errors,
but of the whole theologizing process itself. We must
disentangle religious experience and idealism not only
from dogmas that are old and untrue, but from the whole
concept of dogma. . . . It is the final condemnation of
theology that it tends ever to make religion a contracted
and thus exclusive thing, and shut men off from contact
with their fellows. To find religion is always to find unity,
and therewith a universal fellowship of humankind."

"As the great Reformation went back to Paul, and getting rid of ecclesiasticism, secured liberty, so this new reformation must go back to Jesus. and getting rid of
theology, secure fellowship. It must seek to establish

throughout the world what was established in those early Christian churches in ancient Rome—a solidarity of human interests, a brotherhood of men bound together in love, equal not only in rights but in duties. dedicated in fellowship to the bringing in of God's Kingdom on the earth".

"The Luther of our time will be a social engineer, who will do for love in programs of social change what his immortal predecessor did for faith in creeds of theological belief."

So much for the foregoing viewpoint, that theology must be done away with, and religion socialized.

Let us turn to another form of statement, one that is, shall we say, less radical. or at least just at the moment more representative of liberal tendencies and teaching in nominally orthodox seminaries and churches. The following quotations are from the last chapter of Dr. George A. Coe's "The Religion of a Mature Mind."

"In the spirit of complete intellectual liberty, let us calmly face the question, What if the worst possible. from the doctrinal point of view, should happen? What if we should become fully convinced that the church fathers, the theologians of all ages, and the unnumbered multitude of Christian disciples who have followed the central tradition have been mistaken in their theory about the Christ? Suppose that Jesus was nothing more than a Hebrew prophet of the highest type, who mistakenly applied to himself the Messianic hopes of his people, and was crucified therefor. Suppose that the stories of his miracles and of his resurrection are mere accretions which the uncritical love and enthusiasm of his followers have added to the true history of his life. Complete the case by believing that his character and his teachings have not the moral perfection attributed to them by 'their defenders. Grant that these ideal qualities have been reflected backward upon the name of Jesus from the gradually developing moral consciousness of the Christian world. In a word, suppose that for us the historical Christ were to pass away, leaving only the ideal Christ to cling to."

"Whoever finds the Christ-ideal a supreme one, has firm standing-ground on the positive side, whatever be his state of mind with respect to all else. Granting nothing but the fact of his own approval of the Christ, whether the Christ be merely ideal or also historical, he faces the immediate duty of becoming a worker for the Christian ideal."

"Will not the church some day realize her natural affinity for all souls who thus aspire toward the Christian ideal?"

"A first step in discipleship is taken . . . whenever, convinced of the soundness of the moral idea expressed in the Christ, one accepts the Christ-ideal as one's own."

"Not the affirming of Christ but the experience of Christ is what constitutes the basis of our discipleship."

Somewhat similar in import to the foregoing quotations from Dr. Coe but seemingly more positive, are certain sections in the reply made to Bishop Manning by Dr. Percy S. Grant early in 1923.

"I pass now to my belief in Jesus Christ our Lord. From my heart I believe that Jesus is the Portrait of the Invisible God, the perfect revelation of my Heavenly Father. When I ask myself 'What is God like?' I can only answer, 'He is like Jesus,' and hence I can make my own the words 'He that hath seen Me hath seen the

Father.' But I cannot make my own either Platonist or Aristotelian explanations of the metaphysical relation between our Lord and the Father. I do not know what that metaphysical relationship may be, and I know that no one else on earth knows.''

"With such understanding as I have I am sure that in some sense there was in Jesus an Incarnation of Deity. My entire spiritual experience makes clear to me that His revelation of God is absolutely unique; that He is, as I said above, the very Portrait of the Father. But *how* this was accomplished is to me, from the nature of the case, a wholly speculative question, as to which I know nothing."

"But in thinking of what is called the Deity of Christ, mere intellectual assent or attempted abstract accuracy seems to me to have little value in comparison with ethical allegiance to His teachings. . . . Nearer the ideal and teaching of our Lord, it seems to me, as His ideal and teaching are expressed in our earliest sources, is the thought of the Rev. C. F. Russell, Hulsean lecturer in the Anglican Communion, who, following the ethical conception of the Incarnation so nobly expressed by Athanasius, says:

'Who is it that believes today in the divinity of Christ? Is it not the man whose whole soul goes out in unreserving acceptance of the supremacy of love? Such a definition would include many who do not assume the name of Christian; many who, because they stumble at the creeds, would feel, and might even be told, that they had no place at a Christian Eucharist; many who within the last few years have fought and died for an ideal, for the love of country, for the love of comrades, and yet have stood resolutely outside the churches. Can we doubt that such men acknowledge the Divinity of Christ in the only way in which He would Himself wish such acknowledgment to be made the test of discipleship? The majesty of love has them in thrall.

'There is a negative side to our conclusion as well. However loudly and clearly a man may recite the Creed, he does not really believe this great doctrine of the faith if he does not consciously accept the supremacy of love, whether as revealing the nature of God or as constituting the ideal and principle of true human life. The man who honestly thinks that in the last resort force is mightier than love, whether it be in the affairs of individual men or of nations, does not believe in the Divinity of Christ. The man who deliberately values wealth above opportunity of service, whether for himself or for his friends, does not believe in the Divinity of Christ. In a word, we deny that He is a Divine whenever we set anything save love on the throne of the universe or of the individual heart.' "

It is not our present purpose to criticize in detail either favorably or adversely the positions set forth in the passages quoted in this chapter. Doubtless the reader will already to some extent have passed his own judgment thereon. With much we can sympathize; we can praise the apparent sincerity of all these statements. The writer speaking for himself does not find them complete however or wholly satisfying.

Is there need at present for the discarding of theology in order to socialize religion? Is not the need for more and truer and better theology rather than for less? Is it not necessary to study the religious principles governing our very being, do we not need to ponder upon the relation of man to God, as the very starting point in our consideration of the relation of man to man and justice on the earth? The very idea of justice is theological through and through. Unless we understand something of divine justice, how can we speak of human justice?

Are we satisfied to ascribe to a historic person the attributes of the ideal Christ, as that ideal has been developed through the ages, and make that historic person idealized the center of our religious thought and devotion unless that we believe that the ideal Christ is the real Christ, and unless we feel that he is a present power, even metaphysically if you please, in the universe and in our lives?

And as for belief in the supremacy of love, does this sanction our repetition of the Apostles' Creed, prayer to Jesus, or in the name of Jesus, or statement of belief in his Deity, or his Divinity either, unless this word is so used as to lose its customary and plain every-day meaning?

If you interpret the word divinity in such a way, that you and I can say we believe in the divinity of Isaiah, or of Paul, or of Augustine, or of Lincoln, then I believe in the divinity of Jesus, but not otherwise. We may as well, in fact far better, be plain spoken, and avoid unusual or strained interpretations. The way to truth is through clarity of thought and expression.

"Our guides we pretend must be sinless: as if those were not often the best teachers who only yesterday got corrected for their mistakes." George Eliot.

"That men should have worshipped their poor fellow man as a God, and not him only, but stocks and stones, and all manner of animate and inanimate objects; and fashioned for themselves such a distracted chaos of hallucinations by way of Theory of the Universe: all this looks like an incredible fable. Nevertheless it is a clear fact that they did it. Such hideous inextricable jungle of misworships, misbeliefs, man, made as we are, did actually hold by, and live at home in. This is strange. Yes, we may pause in sorrow and silence over the depths of darkness that are in man: if we rejoice in the heights of purer vision he has attained to. Such things were and are in man; in all men; in us too."

* * * * * *

"In the history of the world there will not again be any man, never so great, whom his fellowmen will take for a god. Nay, we might rationally ask, did any set of human beings ever really think the man they saw there standing beside them a god, the maker of this world? Perhaps not: it was usually some man they remembered. or had seen. But neither can this any more be. The Great Man is not recognized henceforth as a god any more." Carlyle.

"And yet, O Man Born of Woman . . . thy true beginning and Father is in heaven, whom with the bodily eye thou shalt never behold. but only with the spiritual." Carlyle.

The following is from "Sunday in the Mountains: A Meditation" by Charles Edward Garman:

"The thought that has impressed me over and over during the few days of my stay here is this: The strength of the hills is His also: that nature is not something apart from God, but simply the hem of his garment, or rather the veil over His face like that which Moses wore when he came down from the mount where he talked to God face to face. The other thought, companion of this, is the names which have been given to these hills, names which figure prominently in our country's history: Mounts Washington, Jefferson, Adams, Lafayette. What is the sense of this nomenclature? Is a mountain simply a monument to a great man's name, a monument reared by nature instead of by man? This is ridiculous. I feel like apologizing even for the suggestion and yet there is a fitness in the names. Wherein lies the symbolism; is it not this? These mountains were made of common clay, they were once the bed of the ocean, but the great geological forces which shaped our earth and transformed chaos into cosmos lifted them high in air, and gave them a formative influence in determining the climate and fertility of the country at their feet. So our great men in history—men like Washington and Lincoln—were men of the common people. But they were not self-made men. Those great historic forces which have been shaping the destiny of the race brought about the convulsions in our national life that forced them to the front, lifted them high above their fellows, gave them a formative influence in determining the conditions of our national career, and as the mountains drop down the dew, condense the clouds, cool the heated air and send it back laden with balsam odors, and give birth to those streams which have created our mill towns and brought wealth and prosperity where there was only desolation, so have these great men blessed all who came after them, and lived immortal lives. Catching the first beams of the morning sun of reform, and reflecting the last rays of the day whose work is done, their biographies become mountains of our historic life, whither we turn in our partisan troubles and bigoted strifes for that mental vacation, those grand thoughts, that champagne atmosphere of truth, which is the only tonic for a weak mind. And now whence these forces of history, whence these forces of geology, if the strength of the hills is His also? Is not the spirit of the prophet the inspiration of the age? Are not the instincts of human society a power through which God is working to will and to do of His good pleasure in human affairs? Is not this the difference between the old dispensation and the new? Moses received his revelation on tables of stone from the top of Mount Sinai shrouded with clouds and thick darkness. We find God revealed in the lives of our great men; they are our Sinais, and their summits instead of being shrouded with clouds and thick darkness, are lighted up with the light of coming day, and we learn that the strength of the hills is His also."

I hope it will not seem irreverent to any fellow pupil of Professor Garman's, if I apply his beautiful simile between the mountains and the great men in this nation's history, to Jesus. To do so may not represent Professor Garman's thought or belief; I do not for a moment claim that it does. But to me Jesus seems in human history, as Washington or Jefferson or Adams in this nation's life. To me its adds to rather than detracts from our reverent thought to say that like the mountains he was *made of common clay,* but like them has been *lifted high in air* by God Himself and given a *formative influence in determining our spiritual climate* even today. Through him God has worked *to will and to do of His good pleasure in human affairs.*

There is no ground for deification or worship of religious leaders, teachers, or prophets, not even of Jesus.

We do not worship great men in statesmanship, art, discovery, science and industry, or ascribe to them divine honors.

It would seem to be the part of the religious man to *praise God from Whom all blessings flow*.

CHAPTER IV

IS THEOLOGY TO BE CONDEMNED OR DISCARDED?

Theology is not to be condemned or discarded simply because it has so often been faulty or incomplete, or because theologians have not always remembered the great need of humility and charity.

"Christ's discourses were in Aramaic and have come down to us only in translations, some of which are bungling and full of errors, but when he sent his disciples forth as living words on the day of Pentecost he sent a message that did not have to be translated. Parthians and Medes, and Elamites, and the dwellers of Mesopotamia, and Cappadocia, in Pontus, and Asia, strangers of Rome, Jews and proselytes, could all understand lives of heroism and self denying service, for character is the mother tongue of every nation. Those who have long forgotten this native speech are touched when they hear of heroism and devotion as though they listened to the tender accents of home at their mother's knee." Charles E. Garman.

It is indeed well for us that "The blessed work of helping the world forward happily does not wait to be done by perfect men, and I should imagine that neither Luther nor John Bunyan, for example. would have satisfied the modern demand for an ideal hero, who believes nothing but what is true, feels nothing but what is exalted, and does nothing but what is graceful. The real heroes of God's making, are quite different; they have their natural

43

heritage of love and conscience which they drew in their mother's milk; they know one or two of those deep spiritual truths which are only to be won by long wrestling with their own sins and their own sorrows; they have earned faith and strength so far as they have done genuine work; but the rest is dry barren theory, blank prejudice, vague hearsay. Their insight is blended with mere opinion, their sympathy is perhaps confined in narrow conduits of doctrine, instead of flowing forth with the freedom of a stream that blesses every weed in its course." George Eliot.

Even those who most strongly urge return, as it is often expressed, to primitive Christianity, to the simple religion of Jesus, admit that historically the spread of Christianity was largely promoted and influenced by theologians, such as Paul, Augustine, Aquinas, Calvin and Edwards. It is extremely doubtful whether Christianity as a religion would have survived at all without theology. But perhaps it will be said that religion would have survived, and that any way this book is critical of Christianity as a religion.

The writer strongly believes that we are all tremendously indebted to creative theologians, as distinguished from dogmatists. All men theologize to greater or less extent. Theologians have simply studied more thoroughly, thought more deeply and guided and directed the thinking of others. There is constant need for such thought and for such guidance. When theologies become fixed as creeds or dogmas that we are required to accept without or beyond reason, we are right in objecting. Theology like any other science should be free and rest upon reason and not upon arbitrary authority. True theology should bless us with new ideas of the truth, without abandoning what is true in that which we inherit.

"The fate of the poor shepherd, who, blinded and lost in the snow-storm, perishes in a drift within a few feet of his cottage door, is an emblem of the state of man. On the brink of the waters of life and truth, we are miserably dying. The inaccessibleness of every thought but that we are in, is wonderful. What if you come near to it; you are as remote when you are nearest as when you are farthest. . . . Therefore we love the poet, the inventor, who in any form, whether in an ode or in an action or in looks and behavior, has yielded us a new thought. He unlocks our chains and admits us to a new scene." Milton.

The subject matter of theology is well set forth in Carlyle's definition of religion.

"It is well said, in every sense, that a man's religion is the chief fact with regard to him. A man's, or a nation of men's. By religion 1 do not mean here the church creed which he professes, the articles of faith which he will sign and, in words or otherwise, assert; not this wholly, in many cases not this at all. We see men of all kinds of professed creeds attain to almost all degrees of worth or worthlessness under each or any of them. This is not what I call religion. this profession and assertion; which is often only a profession and assertion from the outworks of the man, from the mere argumentative region of him, if even so deep as that. But the thing a man does practically believe (and this is often enough without asserting it even to himself, much less to others) ; the thing a man does practically lay to heart, and know for certain, concerning his vital relations to this mysterious Universe, and his duty and destiny there, that is in all cases the primary thing for him, and creatively determines all the rest. That is his Religion, or it may be, his mere scepticism and *No Religion;* the manner it is in which he feels himself to be spiritually related to the Unseen World or No-World; and I say if you tell me what it is, you tell me to a very great extent what the man is, what the kind of things he will do is."

Just suppose that theology is impossible, and that what calls itself by this name is to be abandoned or destroyed, instead of sought out as one seeks for hidden treasure,— or as it is expressed by F. D. Maurice,—

"Assuredly the idea of an obedience in man, which has no ground to rest upon; which was foreseen by God, but not derived from Him; of something good. therefore, which cannot be traced ultimately to the Fountain of good; nay, which exists independently of it, that is to say, under what are we wont to consider the very condition of evil . . . is a most agonizing contradiction. And what need have we of it? Only do not suppose the Being whom you worship to be a mere power. only acknowledge him to be that in reality which you say in words that He is, the essential truth and goodness; only suppose the absolute will to be a will to good, and how can we imagine that Happiness, Obedience, Freedom, have their origin any where but in Him; that misery, disobedience, slavery, mean anything but revolt and separation from Him?"

Or as the same writer says in another place,

"Now supposing it were possible that truth and goodness are not abstractions, are not formulas, but are realities; and as the traces of them have been seen in the acts of persons, so that they dwell absolutey in a Person; supposing it were true that this Being is the King of kings and Lord of lords, from whom all law derives its life and potency; supposing this Being has established for Himself a witness in the heart of the poorest man in the world, and has decreed that there should be desires in that heart which anything short of his own infinite perfection shall not satisfy; and has called this poor man to be a citizen of his kingdom, yea, a member incorporate thereof, and has said that he, as much as the richest, is concerned in the order and organization of his kingdom, and may urge on the wheels in the midst of which the spirit of the living creature is moving; would it not then be true that cravings of the philosopher, the necessities of the statesman, the hope of the wayfarer, have all their highest interpretation in this worship which is said to be the idlest of ceremonies? Are not the recorded deeds and desires of the world utterly unintelligible without it? If this ceremony were abolished—if the idea of a perfect Being united to man, inspiring him with prayer, and hearing his prayers, were lost out of the universe,—would not the imperfect hope of the philosopher die too? Would not the belief in Law become impossible? Would not each man sink further and further into solitude and brutality, finding none able to raise him, none who was not assisting to deepen his degredation?"

There is before the writer a weekly paper in which a monthly magazine advertises an article on the subject. "Do we need a new religion?"* It is said in the advertisement referred to that the author of the article will say "that Christianity is not accomplishing what was expected

* An advertisement of The Century for September 1923 in Time, September 3, 1923.

of it, that we need a new religion based not on individual
salvation but on the welfare of the groups that compose
modern society." The present writer thoroughly believes
that we need to pass from Christianity to universal religion, but not in order to invent a new religion or simply
for the welfare of social groups. What we need is the
truth,—philosophical truth, theological truth, religious
truth. We live as individuals in relationships. We need
a broader, deeper, truer personal belief before we can
understand or solve social problems. The individual cannot be ignored even for the so-called social good. What
we need is not to invent but to either discover or to re-
discover the fundamental truths of religion. This is the
subject matter of theology, which to be pursued rightly
must be studied with mind and heart and soul.

All great religious teachers have been interested in the
individual and not simply in social progress. They have
felt and taught that each single individual has something
divine within him that is of infinite worth. They have
believed that life is lived by individuals, and that this
fact is not to be ignored.

So Augustine speaks of God as "Almighty Goodness,
who carest for each of us, as if Thou caredst for him
alone, and for all as if they were each alone."

"It was probably a hard saying to the Pharisees, that
there is more joy in heaven over one sinner that repenteth,
than over the ninety-and-nine just persons that need no
repentance. And certain ingenious philosophers of our
own day must surely take offence at a joy so entirely out
of correspondence with arithmetical proportion. . . .
And so it comes to pass that for the man who knows
sympathy because he knows sorrow, that old, old saying

. . . has a meaning that does not jar with the language of his own heart. It only tells him, that for angels too there is a transcendent value in human pain, which refuses to be settled by equations; that the eyes of angels too are turned away from the serene happiness of the righteous to bend with yearning pity on the poor erring soul wandering in the desert where no water is; that for angels too the misery of one casts so tremendous a shadow as to eclipse the bliss of ninety-nine." George Eliot.

Science is search for and study of truth. Theology is that branch of science which deals with the highest and most important phases of truth, those that most thoroughly determine and influence the individual and also through the individual society as a whole. "The truth in its true form is the mightiest thing on earth; it does not need eloquence or skill or passion to plead its claims; it makes way for itself; rises upon mankind as the unclouded sun does upon the earth, and puts the earth under the sense of its glory and beneficent power." (Dr. George A. Gordon.)

Some commonly urged objections to theology, and discussion of its method, with remarks as to present day practical problems remain to be considered. Before taking up such questions, however, a chapter is inserted that expresses far better than the present writer himself could do a plea for theology.

Thomas Carlyle wrote, "It is not necessary a man should himself have discovered the truth he is to believe in, and never so sincerely believe in. . . . The merit of originality is not novelty; it is sincerity. The believing man is the original man; whatsoever he believes, he believes it for himself, not for another."

CHAPTER V

A PLEA FOR THEOLOGY

(This chapter is comprised entirely of quotations from an address by Charles Edward Garman entitled, "A Plea for Philosophy in the Pulpit," which was delivered by Professor Garman before the Yale Divinity School and as Carew Lecture before the Hartford Theological Seminary, both in 1898. The reader is referred to the full address,* which the quotations here presented but summarize.)

"No doubt the mere statement of this topic will awaken in the minds of some of you serious questioning. You will ask, Does not this amount to a plea for rationalism? Has not metaphysics always been a stumbling block to weak faith. and a source of skepticism and irreligion? Can any good thing come out of philosophy?

"To this inquiry I must beg leave to give the Scriptural reply, 'Come and see.' "

* * * * * *

"It is claimed that the mainspring of human action is not knowledge, but impulse. It is not a lack of philosophy that prevents men from doing right, but their slavery to passion. . . . Suppose a city should build a large hospital and fill it with patients in advanced stages of disease: but the city fathers, instead of employing the

---

* "Letters, Lectures and Addresses of Charles Edward Garman,—A Memorial Volume" published by Houghton Mifflin Co.—pages 408 and following.

best nurses and medical assistance, should hire the most expert investigators and professors to read to those at the point of death learned lectures on physiology, and long tables of statistics on hygiene and athletics. Would this, it is asked, be more ridiculous than for the church to place in its pulpits expounders of philosophy instead of preachers of the gospel?

"The truth is, claims the objector that sinful human nature can be benefited by no other help than that of the Great Physician. . . . The preacher is not a philosopher but a minister plenipotentiary from the court of heaven, through whom the divine negotiations are conducted and the divine assistance is offered. He speaks not by his own authority nor by the will of man; if his message be not from God it is naught. . . .

"The Christian preacher is a commissioner sent out from God with God's emancipation proclamation to sinful men. In the days of the Apostles, to preach meant simply to herald; to announce with authority the glad tidings, the gospel of divine intervention, and it is claimed that the apostles in every age can have no other mission.

"You will ask what I have to say to this conception of a preacher's function.

"In reply, I would give three answers. First: It seems to me a pity that those who grasp with such clearness this great truth concerning the divine plan of salvation, and who thereby show such a keenness of insight into the limitations of human nature that all true students of social problems might well envy them—it seems to me such a pity that these persons should make the great mistake of supposing that this is the only truth in the Bible, and that the only need of sinful men is that of the new birth, and of help to overcome passion. These religious workers who spend all their efforts in converting men, and getting them to unite with the church, and then leave them to shift for themselves in the religious life, make a very near approach to adopting the methods which Spain has followed in dealing with non-combatants in Cuba. Such converts are little better than spiritual reconcentradoes, and they excite our pity in the extreme."

*   *   *   *   *   *

"To put the question concretely: Is it possible for us to truly worship God, that is, reverence and adore Him and be inspired by His perfections unless we can in some measure come into a knowledge of Him and His work? . . . It is sometimes claimed that mystery is essential to religion, and that if the mysteries could be removed it would be taking away our reverence; that a God understood would be no God at all. But I beg leave to ask you to what are you looking forward in your future life? To a period of greater mystery, or, with the Apostle Paul, do you say, 'Then shall I know even as I am known?' Will the sanctity, the love and the adoration of worshipers in the New Jerusalem be diminished by this increase of knowledge? Must not the law of life which holds in heaven hold on earth? Therefore in proportion as we reach out towards that larger knowledge of God, is not the light of that other world breaking upon the hilltops of this life with its morning splendor? This is the aim of philosophy, and I feel that to this end the preacher must strive if the Spirit speaks through him to the church.

"My second answer is the claim that if the mere preaching of the fact of an atonement was sufficient formerly

to persuade men to repent and be born again, it is no
longer adequate." . . .

* * * * * *

"The public at large are beginning to feel that there
is no dividing line between time and eternity, the here
and the hereafter; that a man's character will be governed
by exactly the same laws, no matter how changed his environment may be. From a scientific point of view, then
men determine the value of religion by its influence upon
the present life. If not essential for the life that now is,
they ask what evidence do we have that it will be of any
avail hereafter? On the other hand, if you can show us
that it is the mainspring of existence here, we will trust
it now, and we will trust it for the future also. If we
desire to save men we must go to them where they are
and not wait for them to come to us. This forces the
preacher to meet men on a scientific basis."

* * * * * *

"My third answer is that just at present certain false
conceptions of God and duty, indeed, of life in general,
are so prevalent that men are now biased against the
gospel. They will not hear when you simply preach the
fact of redemption. . . . Whatever may be true of
men's creed, nothing is clearer than the fact that the personality and sovereignty of God are not a large factor in
the practical life and thought of our age."

* * * * * *

"I can discover but one remedy for this state of affairs.
The church must not merely affirm the personality of
God—for to many this would be a mere formula—the
church must help men realize the divine personality; it
must force men to see that personality and sovereignty

are the supreme facts of the universe. But this cannot be done unless you philosophize.

"But, you say, surely you do not expect us to turn professors and teach Kant and Wundt to our congregations as a part of our divine message. Is anything more unintelligible than the abstract formulae of such writers, or more confusing, and to a popular mind, more absurd, than their conclusions? Common men have no trouble in apprehending the external world and the great facts of every-day life, but philosophers make easy things hard and puzzle their brains over problems that do not exist—at least this is so in the material world. If they stumble so here, ought we to wonder that they 'go all to pieces' over spiritual reality? To the ordinary man they are blind leaders of the blind; how can you ask us to impose on our congregations such leadership?

"In reply to this question let me say a few words in behalf of the much-abused philosophers.

"It is not difficult for orators and newspapers to raise the loud laugh at their expense. We confess that their terminology is often difficult, and their doctrines at first sight appear very contradictory, but what Macauley said in defense of the Puritans holds also of them: 'It is not from the laughers alone that the truth is to be learned.' We may paraphrase still further from Macauley and say, The ridiculous part of their work is on the surface. He who runs may read. But most of their peculiarities are mere external badges, like the signs of Free Masonry or the dress of the friars. We regret that these badges are not more attractive; we regret that a body of men to whose courage and talents mankind has owed inestimable obligations, have not always had the lofty elegance of style which distinguishes novelists and dramatists, or the easy wit for which after-dinner speakers are so often celebrated. But we must make our choice; we will, like Bassanio in the play, turn from the specious caskets of gold and silver which often contain only the death's head and the fool's head, and fix on the small, plain leaden chest of philosophy which holds civilization's great treasure, truth.

"Some time ago a student expressed his estimate of . . . philosophy in these words: 'Bricks without straw, but plenty of mud, though'." . . .

"But if one were not making a campaign of criticism, if one were really in earnest in his search for truth, he would find this so-called mud very different stuff from what it first appeared to be. He would find it composed of ingredients quite as marvelous as those Ruskin found in the mud of a manufacturing village. . . . He says: 'Beginning with the clay. Leave it still quiet to follow its own instinct of unity, and it becomes not only white but clear, not only clear but hard, not only clear and hard, but so set that it can deal with the light in a wonderful way and gather out of it the loveliest blue rays only, refusing the rest. We call it then sapphire.'

"Then he takes the sand and, under similar conditions, finds it arranging itself in such a form that it has the power to reflect not merely the blue rays, but blue, green, purple, and red in the greatest beauty in which they can be seen through any hard material whatsoever. We call it then an opal.

"Encouraged by these discoveries, Ruskin sets himself to examine what seems to be the filthy soot. It cannot make itself white at first, but, instead of being discouraged.

tries harder and harder and comes out at last the hardest thing in the world; in exchange for the blackness that it had, it obtains the power of reflecting all the rays of the sun at once in the vividest blaze that any solid thing can shoot.   We call it then a diamond.   The ounce of slime which we despised has, under favorable conditions, become three of the most precious jewels—a sapphire, an opal, and a diamond.

"In a similar manner those difficult and confusing philosophical treatises, with their repulsive terminology, that seem so absurd on their first reading, will, if time and thought are given to them by a candid mind, crystallize into the most precious truths that have ever rewarded the search of a finite human being.   It is just these truths, in their crystallized form, that preachers need to make accessible to their congregations in this age of criticism and reconstruction.   Among the great truths thus brought within our reach are these three:

"First, Idealism; or the conception of the universe, material as truly as moral, as dependent on God for its continued existence from moment to moment, as truly as the rainbow on the continued shining of the sun.   Philosophy takes literally Christ's words, that not a sparrow falls to the ground 'without your Father.'   So also the words of the Apostle Paul: 'For in Him we live, and move, and have our being'.

"Secondly, the conception of Personality is the ultimate fact of the universe.   From which it follows that all nature as truly as all human history has not merely a scientific, but also an ethical and a religious, import, and is progressing towards the realization of divine ideals.   This is the foundation for all true optimism.   Philosophy deals with practical pantheism by tracing it to its sources. All our best thinkers agree that the mainspring of life is not intelligence, but feelings and will, or, technically, impulse.

"But two positions are quite possible on this basis. First, man has two kinds of impulse. Those that are animal, and work blindly, like instinct, and those that are spiritual, which can realize themselves only through clear, though not necessarily formulated, cognitions.

"The second position denies this fundamental distinction. It affirms that all our impulses, both animal and spiritual, are akin to instinct and act blindly except where they encounter resistance. Just as electricity runs along a good conductor without giving any evidence of its presence, but is converted into light and heat by the resistance of the carbons, so it is only where our impulse experiences certain antagonism that it awakens conscious thought and reflection.

"This view makes personality the transient phase of life, due to peculiar antagonism in our nature, and thus an indication of imperfection. We can think of man as personal now, but he must be tending towards a state when his individual consciousness will disappear. All progress will be illustrated by those kinds of action, like articulation, elocution, or the mastery of a foreign language, which require the most painful effort at the beginning, but which, when thoroughly mastered, become wholly automatic and drop into unconsciousness. It would not be considered an exhibition of culture for one to have to stop in an oration to think of his grammar, or, in society, to study out of his etiquette. Perfection here is unconsciousness; and if all life corresponds to these types, the same must be true of our virtue and of our re-

ligion. Indeed, the highest success would be impossible
to one who depends on calculation. Either human beings
cannot think at all, or the conceptions they apply to men
must be the standards by which they judge of God. Our
mental processes are exactly the same whether we think
about divine things or about human affairs. It follows
that if personality, intelligence, consciousness is a transi-
tional stage with men, it cannot be attributed to God.
He must be perfect, therefore He must have advanced
beyond this stage of existence.

"A true philosophy lays the axe at the root of this tree.
It recognizes clearly that spiritual impulses are not blind.
but can act only through intelligence. Then perfection of
life will consist in perfection of knowledge and personality ;
then it will be impossible to think of the Divine Being as
other than omniscient, the tender, loving Father. Impersonal law will give place to the liberty of the sons of
God. This is the only true view. Take Longfellow's
Evangeline. The impulse to follow her lover through
all these years of wandering is indeed the mainspring of
her action, but can this impulse, acting blindly, find him?
Is there a more pathetic scene in literature than when,
floating down the Ohio River, her party lands on an is-
land for rest. in the middle of the day. at the very time
when her lover is rowing by on the other side? The animal impulse to rest can execute itself without intelligence.
When Evangeline was tired she could drop to sleep
without understanding the processes involved in slumber ;
she could take a reclining position without knowing the
physiological principles which required it, for these animal
impulses are as blind and automatic as magnetism which
turns the needle to the pole. Had her spiritual impulse

of devotion to her lover been of this type she would have moved towards him as unconsciously as a stone falls towards the earth. But because the spiritual impulses could only be guided by intelligence, and she knew not what was going on about her, she embarks again, and every hour carries her farther and farther in the direction opposite to that taken by her lover.

"What is true here is true in the religious life, if we do not add to our faith knowledge in the services of God. We need a philosophy of the divine life to fit our own actions into the course of events and make our lives count in our generation."

* * * * * *

"The great doctrine of Sovereignty is the third of the jewels that crystallize out of philosophical discussions. This is something infinitely more than mere cause and effect. It is the ultimate principle of all personal relationship, not merely between God and man, but quite as much between man and his fellows. Philosophy shows that human government and divine government stand or fall together. We cannot hold to the former and deny the latter. If God is not sovereign over man, then surely no finite human being, or collection of human beings called the State, has any right to exercise sovereignty over unwilling subjects; all true government is therefore sacred. But there is no government where there are no sanctions to the law. for then laws become mere advice. When men realize this, the fact of an atonement is their only hope for mercy.

"Having spoken of the subject-matter with which philosophy is concerned and of its great value to the preacher, let me now speak of the methods of work employed in philosophy—of the processes. You will better understand why philosophy is so easily misjudged; but you will also clearly see that these methods are sure in time to receive large recognition.

"The philosopher is a man who has discovered that the real meaning and value of things can be accurately determined only as we judge *the part in the light of the whole;* he lays emphasis on the fact that, if we have a wrong idea of the whole, we distort, and oftentimes make meaningless, the parts; therefore he makes a special effort to look at things, especially at religious things, comprehensively and accurately.

"It will be seen thus that philosophy is simply *intelligence* at its best. All intelligence works backward; even in trivial matters we have to start with the knowledge of the end before we can determine the means. The builder of an humble dwelling-house must have an idea of the finished structure before he is able to break the ground and lay the foundations."

* * * * * *

"But if we must deal with even *trivial* things in this way, can we be intelligent if we do not follow the same methods in apprehending larger affairs? The idea that the universe in which we live is a whole—the notion that mind and matter, history and revelation, church and state, time and eternity, are not separate wholes, but parts that somehow fit into each other, and can be understood only in relationship to the grand end they serve—this is the idea both of philosophy and of religion, and is coming to be the view of science itself."

* * * * * *

"But it is objected that philosophy is too abstract to

be of assistance to the church. We reply, those who call
themselves plain, common-sense people, and not the philosopher, are guilty of abstraction, and live in an ideal or
imaginary universe. This is evident when you remember
that an abstraction is the separating in thought that which
is not, or cannot be, separated in reality. It is the taking
of a part as a little whole by itself, instead of looking at
it in its true relationship to the larger whole, as philosophy
demands."

*   *   *   *   *   *

"If a steel needle is something so grand, so wonderful,
that the most thorough scientific study has not yet begun
to conceive aright its real nature, if there is such a hidden
depth of meaning and miracle in its motions, can you
blame the philosopher for pausing, with reverence and
awe, in his study of a finite human mind, even though it
be that of a mere child? Is he abstract and visionary
when he asks how much is potential to the humblest human
being, what are his hidden spiritual powers?"   .   .   .

*   *   *   *   *   *

"Only as the preacher employs these processes and can
present this point of view to his audience can he lift them
to a level where they will grasp the divine estimate that
man is made 'only a little lower than the angels,' and
crowned with honor and everlasting life; that 'the redemption of the humblest is worth the life of the Son of
God.' Only from this point of view can our modern
civilization realize in any adequate manner the exceeding
sinfulness of sin, or truly reverence and worship the
author of man's being."

*   *   *   *   *   *

"Truth shines the brightest in just such a time as the

present. Philosophy is something like astronomy, in that night is a peculiarly favorable time to make observations. Had the sun always been above the horizon, we should have had no astronomy, and Columbus would never have learned to pilot his way across unknown seas to America. For stars there would have been none, and without these we never could have divined the mysteries of the heavens or the revelation of the earth. 'A dome of blue lighted by a single torch; an irregular plain of sand and water' would ever have remained our universe. Astronomy was born of superstition (astrology) and cradled in the dark.

"Philosophy had a similar birth. It did not originate in the immediate light of revelation. Had men always dwelt in the dread mysterious presence of oracles and miracles, had there been no ominous silence. no darkness that might be felt; men had never dreamed of that firmament of thought wherein arise and shine the truths of the eternal. They would still be looking for God in the heavens above, or in the earth beneath; they would not easily find Him in the still small voice, in that holy of holies in our hearts."

*   *   *   *   *   *

"Has not the church a duty to society and to the state in these troubled times? Ought it not to aim to make good citizens, and be wholly the ally of reform? Have we not reached, or nearly reached, a stage in the development of civilization when further progress will require exact comprehension of the great principles that dominate man's spiritual nature? In early times business success was a matter of happy guesswork. Men did not stop to figure out the cost of raw materials, of transportation. of manufacturing, and of commissions, as is now done.

Mathematics then was merely a business luxury, the margin of profits was so large. But the time came when mathematics became a necessity; when only the most exact bookkeeping and the most accurate precision could prevent disaster.

"Is not a similar change taking place in the social and political world? In the complex organization of modern life, can we longer trust to happy guesses; can we blindly try costly experiments to reform present evils? If I read aright the signs of the time, the day is not far distant when our social and political questions, and our international relations, will be recognized as much profounder problems than many are now willing to admit." . . .

* * * * * *

"Why should not the time come when statesmen should feel that for the improvement of government and society, there is imperatively needed the guidance of those great spiritual truths, those spiritual laws that a true philosophy reveals? But God's government over man is confessedly the incarnation of just these truths and just these laws. It is an object lesson as to how man should govern his fellow-man. Why, then, should not the philosophy of religion in time be as highly prized by our social reformers as is the philosophy of education by our great educators?

"These problems have an economic side; but they are primarily infinitely more than that: and any attempt to settle them on an economic foundation is an attempt to build on the sand. Such questions as are involved in socialism, for instance, in criminology and penology, in marriage and divorce, and even in municipal reform, are at their foundation religious questions. They can be satisfactorily adjusted only when they conform to the great principles which find expression in the Kingdom of God on earth."

*   *   *   *   *   *

"It is only by the regeneration of mankind—it is only when the state, and institutions, as truly as individuals, are born again, and the reign of righteousness and love, that is, self-sacrifice, shall be established, that the age of universal peace will dawn upon us. The true philosophy of man's spiritual nature puts its whole emphasis upon these facts, and surely the preacher can do greater service to his age than to give his congregation spiritual insight into the religious principles at the foundation of society."

CHAPTER VI

THE THEOLOGICAL APPROACH

All too often in theological discussion or in forming our opinions as to men and beliefs we are inclined to label a man or an opinion rather than to consider the question at issue impartially. Some men and some churches delight in the term conservative or orthodox; others equally delight in change, and the name of liberal or radical. Why do we need such labels? If there is any choice the term conservative seems to be preferable; there is so much in all the past that is worth conserving. But we can not afford or dare to be less progressive than science. None the less will every sincere man believe in proving all things and holding fast to that which is good.

What greater prayer can any man offer than that which has come down from Chrysostom, "Grant us in this world knowledge of Thy truth, and in the world to come life everlasting." The truth in itself is neither conservative nor orthodox on the one side nor radical nor revolutionary on the other, but just the truth. At one time and in one place he who follows the truth may need to hold to it against unwise and foolish change. He will then appear as a conservative. At another time or under different circumstances he who follows truth may find it necessary to seek change from evil and falsehood or at least from outgrown creeds. and to seek for essentials, to get at the root of pending questions. Such a man then seems radical or revolutionary.

The truth itself however is just the truth. Why be-cloud issues by using labels or form our opinions on the basis of adjectives?

"For mankind faith is the one thing needful."* So earnestly do all men love belief and hate scepticism and doubt, that, as we may see on every hand, they are dis-posed to cling to beliefs of days gone by, long after these beliefs have ceased to be soul-compelling for them. No-where are we more conservative by nature than in our re-ligious beliefs. Nor is it to be wondered at that we should jealously guard these beliefs. They are well worth guard-ing because so far as they are good they are our heritage from God Himself, which we have received at His hand through the greatest and the best of men, and which have been enshrined in multitudes of saintly lives, and hallowed by sufferings of prophets and martyrs, and heroes in-numerable.

We instinctively feel it to be a kind of sacrilege when some second or third rate thinker attacks with sarcasm or with ridicule such great teachers as Isaiah, or Jesus, or Paul, or Augustine, or Aquinas or Calvin or Edwards. We rightly feel that the critic ought first to have been the loving disciple and then if possible continue the work of his master, building upon the foundation already laid. Or if it should perchance be at some crisis when it seems necessary to raze the old structure before the new can be erected, even the more strictly is the old New England test insisted upon by us all. "If any who are given to change do rise up to unhinge the well established churches in this land, it will be the duty and interest of the churches

---

* Carlyle.

to examine whether the men of this trepass are more prayerful, more watchful, more zealous, more patient, more heavenly, more universally conscientious, and harder students, and better scholars and more willing to be informed and advised than those great and good men who left unto the churches what they now enjoy."

Perhaps the writer is unduly proud of the old New England Congregational churches. The foregoing quotation, it will be observed, while it stands firmly against unwise or heedless and restless change, recognizes the need and possibility of progress. If we say that one who changes his creed ought to leave his church, creeds could never be changed, or churches progress, except by revolutionary means, and this puts creeds above those who fashioned them. The makers of creeds or those whom they follow, were innovators. In a word, by no right whatsoever has any church warrant for adoption of a final and definite creed as a test of membership. To do so is to place the creed above man, and to close the way to larger and fuller truth. Creeds have their place as expressions of present belief but they are always subject to change and are not or should not be obligatory upon any. The moment a creed ceases to be believed it should not be used by the unbeliever. But this is no reason why one must leave the church, unless the church becomes unworthy of the name by attempting to shut out from itself seekers after truth. The way to truth is the way of an open mind.

There do come times when it is necessary for one who prefers truth to favor of men, or reality to appearance, to attack, and that in no uncertain way, those beliefs whence in days gone by he himself has received nurture and life. Nor should difficulties nor the consciousness of his own weakness and sin, lend excuse to his desire for ease, but he ought valiantly to stand for freedom against all comers, on behalf of those things that he does know and has been persuaded of, and has come to believe in with mind and heart and soul, and has tested in life and experience. Nor does fear of disturbing the beliefs of others justify silence in the court where truth is on trial. Every witness, and the advocates are responsible, not for the effects of the truth, but for the spirit and the method in which they present it.

"The thing is untrue, we were traitors against the Giver of all Truth, if we durst pretend to think it true. Away with it ; . . . Luther and his Protestantism is not responsible for wars. . . Luther did what every man that God has made has not only the right, but lies under sacred duty to do ; answered a Falsehood when it questioned him, Dost thou believe me ?—No !—At what cost soever, without counting of costs, this thing behooved to be done." Carlyle.

At present we are at a time of religious crisis. That there have been very considerable changes in theology all will readily grant, but few who have not especially investigated the subject, realize the scope and the depth of these changes. Even the most careless observer however cannot have failed to note the frequent discussions as to whether the church is losing influence, or why more men do not actively associate themselves therewith, or why young men of ability so seldom consider the ministry in the choice of a life work.

In estimating the influence of the church it is first of all requisite that we have a clear conception of its primary work, which is beyond all debate to teach men of God and

bring them to Him. Dr. Lyman Abbott spoke of religion
as "the life of God in the soul of man".

The church is not a business institution for the earning
of profits, nor an athletic club for the training of men's
bodies, nor a school for the training of men for industrial
or professional life; it is not a hospital, nor even a charit-
able institution. Neither is it a political organization for
the promotion of good government. It is not a lecture.
room for current discussion, nor does it take the place of
the daily or the weekly press. It is not a social settlement,
nor a center for social intercourse; it is not an art museum
nor a musical institute. The church is a religious institution. In any discussion therefore as to whether the church
is at present advancing or going backward. it is essential
that we keep in mind what we mean by a church. For
example, it is conceivable that a church might install a
large gymnasium, organize musical and social clubs, and
by discussion of political and current topics, and by lectures on art and literature build up a large plant, and fill
its walls with an ever increasing throng. Suppose, however, this particular church should practically confine itself to these lines of activity and neither point men to God
or teach them of Him, and of the religious principles at
the foundation of all human relationships, in a word suppose the leaders conceived of a church primarily as a club
or institution for the service of man in promotion of physical, mental, and aesthetic well-being, would it be a case
in evidence of the influence of the church to cite the prosperity of this organization? Quite the contrary, for however useful and wise it may be in particular instances to
engage in these activities, and no church can neglect some
or all of them, the position of the church in any commun-

ity must ultimately come back to the question of its religious influence. And it is right here that the Protestant church is at present most weak and in the opinion of the writer, well-nigh a complete failure. In the writer's opinion the reason for this state of affairs is that the teaching of so many churches, so-called liberal, is either negative or at least lacking in positive belief, while on the other hand in so-called orthodox churches, where the teaching may be positive enough, it does not square with men's beliefs and experience and is contrary to science and to what is accepted outside of the church.

Some time ago in conversation, a friend, who had attended two of the leading theological seminaries of the country, suggested that these institutions were dispensers of negative knowledge. Nor is this a service of no value. Well could it be said to a certain clergyman, who remarked that he believed he had not lost anything, in view of this, by non-attendance at a seminary, "Yes, you have, you have lost important negative knowledge; you believe a whole lot of things that are not so"

My friend however has suggested that it is a great pity that it takes the seminaries so long to give us this negative knowledge. It would be better if they would print a list of things that are not so, and give to each student upon entrance, and then, if they cannot help him with positive beliefs, at least leave him free to attempt to work out his own salvation, instead of taking up all his time in teaching him the negative side.

Broadly speaking, present day churches fall into one of three classes :—

(1) those that strictly speaking are not churches but clubs of one kind or other as aforementioned,

(2) those that teach things that are not so,

(3) dispensers of negative knowledge.

The second class is comprised of orthodox churches whose doctrines are impossible of real and hearty belief on the part of many persons. The third class embraces the more liberal of the nominally orthodox churches and most Unitarian churches.

Compelled to choose between these two classes the modern man is indeed in a sad position. If he is un-educated or non-progressive or has not sensed the contra-diction between traditional theology and science, religion may perhaps be held as a thing apart from the rest of life; or if early training has not been seriously called into question by the developments of his later life, or if his feelings get the better of his reason, he can perhaps find real strength and help in the strictly orthodox churches. Otherwise he can hope for little from the church, unless he is so fortunate as to find one of those which are few and far between, where there is no conflict between head and heart, but a message of life which may be accepted with both mind and soul. All too often, however, the re-sult is indifference, and outward conformity with at best only half-hearted belief.

This book is an attempt to outline at least an approach to the method and an answer to the question not simply what may we, but what must we believe about the great-est things, about God, man, and man's relation to God and to his fellow men. I have included some sections, or at least one chapter, that entitled *A Criticism of Mod-ern Theology* which in effect is a chapter on *Negative Knowledge*, in order that we may be free to pursue our course with clearer understanding and in more perfect light, unhampered by lurking ideas or impossible solutions to our problems.

It may be objected that theological discussion is at best barren of results and that at worst it separates and divides men. It may be objected that in times past differences in creed have caused or been the occasion of wars and of discord, that what we need is fellowship and union through abandonment of discusison on these subjects, that by compromise or at least by silence, and dropping of these questions which divide, we should unite in social service.

It may be put forward that it is a glory of our country that there is freedom of religious belief and we had best let every one go his own way as he sees fit as far as theology and religion are concerned.

We also would join hands with those who preach charity and the right and duty of individual judgment, and that we should allow every man to follow the dictates of his own conscience in matters of religion. But this does not imply that progress is made by compromise. The only lasting unity is unity in the truth and the way to knowledge of the truth is through discussion in the spirit of sincere open-mindedness, charity and mutual respect. We cannot respect the one who compromises on a vital matter of truth or uses false means even in a good cause.

The philosopher Kant well stated the case in the following passages:

"There is in human nature a certain disingenuousness which, however, like everything that springs from nature, must contain a useful germ, namely a tendency to conceal one's true sentiments. and to give expression to adopted opinions which are supposed to be good and creditable.

There is no doubt that this tendency to conceal one's self and to assume a favourable appearance has helped towards the progress of civilization, nay to a certain extent, of morality, because others, who could not see through the varnish of respectability, honesty, and correctness, were led to improve themselves by seeing everywhere these examples of goodness which they believed to be genuine. This tendency, however, to show oneself better than one really is, and to utter sentiments which one does not really share, can only serve provisionally to rescue men from a rude state, and to teach them to assume at least the appearance of what they know to be good. Afterwards, when genuine principles have once been developed and become part of our nature, that disingenuousness must be gradually conquered, because it will otherwise deprave the heart and not allow the good seeds of honest conviction to grow up among the tares of fair appearances.

"I am sorry to observe the same disingenuousness, concealment, and hypocrisy even in the utterances of speculative thought, though there are here fewer hindrances in uttering our convictions openly and freely as we ought, and no advantage whatever in our not doing so. For what can be more mischievous to the advancement of knowledge than to communicate even our thoughts in a falsified form to conceal doubts which we feel in our own assertions, and impart an appearance of conclusiveness to arguments which we know ourselves to be inconclusive? So long as these tricks arise from personal vanity only (which is commonly the case with speculative arguments, as touching no particular interests, nor easily capable of apodictic certainty) they are mostly counteracted by the vanity of others, with the full approval of the public at large, and thus the result is generally the same as would or might have been obtained sooner by means of pure ingenuousness and honesty.   But where the public has once persuaded itself that certain subtle speculators aim at nothing less than to shake the very foundations of the common welfare of the people, it is supposed to be not only prudent, but even advisable and honorable, to come to the succor of what is called the good cause, by sophistries, rather than to allow to our supposed antagonists the satisfaction of having lowered our tone to that of a purely practical conviction, and having forced us to confess the absence of all speculative and apodictic certainty.   I cannot believe this, nor can I admit that the intention of serving a good cause can ever be combined with trickery, misrepresentation, and fraud.   That in weighing the arguments of a speculative discussion we ought to be honest, seems the least that can be demanded ; and if we could at least depend on this with perfect certainty, the conflict of speculative reason with regard to the important questions of God, the immortality of the soul, and freedom, would long ago have been decided, or would soon be brought to a conclusion.   Thus it often happens that the purity of motives and sentiments stands in an inverse ratio to the goodness of the cause, and that its supposed assailants are more honest and straightforward than its defenders."

"It is part of that freedom that we should be allowed openly to state our thoughts and our doubts which we cannot solve ourselves, without running the risk of being decried, on that account as turbulent and dangerous citizens.   This follows from the inherent rights of reason which recognizes no other judge but universal human reason itself. Here everybody has a vote; and, as all improvements of which our state is capable must spring from thence. such rights are' sacred and must never be minished. Nay, it would really be foolish to proclaim certain bold assertions, or reckless attacks upon assertions which enjoy the approval of the largest and best portion of the commonwealth, as dangerous; for that would be to impart to them an importance which they do not possess. Whenever I hear that some uncommon genius has demonstrated away the freedom of the human will, the hope of a future life, or the existence of God, I am always desirous to read his book, for I expect that his talent will help me to improve my own insight into these problems."

There is no greater error than in thinking that truth and pursuit of truth divide men. We now have sects and religions instead of one religion, because men accept tradition rather than the spirit of freedom, light, and truth. There is unity among sincere and open-minded men; however much they may differ as to conclusions they are at one in principles and in methods. It is as true today in the realm of the spiritual as it was of this nation when Abraham Lincoln said it could not remain half slave and half free.

The New Testament teaches us that the truth shall make us free. "Ye shall know the truth, and the truth shall make you free." John 8: 32.

"If all wars, civil and other, are misunderstandings, what a thing right understanding must be!" Carlyle.

"The exercise of private judgment. faithfully gone about, does by no means necessarily end in selfish independence, isolation; but rather ends necessarily in the opposite of that. It is not honest enquiry that makes anarchy; but it is error, insincerity, half-belief and untruth that make it. A man protesting against error is on the way towards uniting himself with all men that believe in truth. There is no communion possible among men who believe only in hearsays. The heart of each is lying dead; has no power of sympathy even with things,—or he would believe them and not hearsays. No sympathy even with things; how much less with his fellow-men! He cannot unite with men; he is an anarchic man. Only in a world of sincere men is unity possible;—and there, in the long-run, it is as good as certain." Carlyle.

If it is true that God is one, and religion is one, will not theology rightly pursued promote unity among men, as nothing else will do?

"Human nature is a country like Holland; it is below the sea level of superstition. The tidal wave of fancticism has rolled over human history again and again, wrecking all that was fair and promising and leaving behind only death and moral pestilence. Against this terrible disaster there is only one protection. We must build dikes around human nature, and the only dikes that will stand will be those constructed on evidence. Then men live in peace and safety. He who destroys these dikes is the arch traitor of the race. He is attempting to again flood humanity with passion and credulity." Garman.

The following is an extract from a published letter of Professor Garman to President Hall of Clark University, regarding the methods followed in his classes in philosophy at Amherst College. (See American Journal of Psychology, Vol. IX, 1898).

"But when the idea fairly dawns upon them (i. e., the

students) that true scholarship consists, not in some mystical quality of genius which ordinary men do not possess, but in simple honesty to one's self in following out the Cartesian Golden Rule, then they experience a new birth, they are no longer boys or slaves, but men. If they attain citizenship in the kingdom of truth, they perceive that the difference between the greatest and the smallest consists only in the quickness and comprehensiveness and thoroughness and humility of their work. Truth to one man is truth to all if they can get exactly the same data and exactly the same standards. Henceforth they call no man master or lord, for all are brethren."

Centuries ago Augustine wrote:

"I did not understand that God is a spirit, who has no parts that can be measured, whose being is not a bulk, because bulk is less in the part than in the whole, and, even if it be infinite, is less in some definite portion than in its infinity, and cannot be wholly everywhere like God, who is spirit. And I had not the least conception in what we are like God, or whether Scripture was right in saying that we are in the image of God. Nor did I know the true inner righteousness, which judges not conventionally but by the upright law of God, whereby the customs of countries and times are adapted to the countries and times, though the law is the same everywhere and always. I did not see that by this law Abraham and Isaac and Jacob and Moses and David and all who are praised by the mouth of God were righteous; though they were counted unrighteous by foolish men, judging by man's day, and measuring the morality of the whole human race by the petty rule of their own morality, just as if one, who knew nothing about armour should fasten a greave on his head and shoe his foot with a helmet, and then complain because they do not fit; or as if when a holiday has been proclaimed for the afternoon, he should make a disturbance because he may not open his shop after twelve o'clock though it was lawful in the morning; or as if in some great household, having discovered that one slave was allowed to handle things which the butler might not touch, or that things might be done in the stable which was forbidden in the dining room, he should make angry complaints, that in one house and in one family all have not the same office at the same time.

"Such are they who are indignant, when they hear that some things were lawful for the righteous in old times, which are not permitted now; or that God for temporary reasons gave the ancients one commandment, us another, though we both obey the same righteousness; or when they see that in one man, in one day, in one house, different offices suit different members, that what was right just now was not right when the clock has struck, that what is done, nay, must be done, in one room is properly forbidden and punished in another. Is justice then capricious or unchangeable? No, but the times, over which justice presides, do not run evenly, because they are times. So men, whose days upon the earth are few, quarrel with the past and accept the present, because they cannot actually see the connection between the laws that governed ages and nations of old and these that are now in operation: while they can individuals, days, houses, in which different things at different moments are suitable to different members, parts, or persons."

At present it is the fashion to decry theology. The writer believes this a grave error, and the chief reason why the churches make so little appeal to men. By discarding theology there has been taken from religion its hold upon all phases of life and its relation to science and history. As a result religion seems a thing apart from life. The great theologians of the past are those who have united in themselves the religious, philosophical and historical beliefs of their times, and by interrelating them and by search for consistency have transformed and correlated and corrected them, so that as a unified whole they could inspire and guide their own lives and the lives of others. New discoveries, progress of science, and new views as to history, bring the demand for new correlation and correction. No one denies for example that Jonathan Edwards was a great theologian. But how greatly has man's whole outlook upon life and the world, past, present and future, changed since his time. It is an error however to believe that his entire theology is of no value, rather does it need to be restated in the light of new knowledge.

There is a great deal of truth in the following from the preface of Dr. George A. Gordon's book entitled "The Christ of Today." The present writer quotes this as illustrative of the general problem rather than as applying to Edwards only. We might in a measure write similarly of Calvin and of Augustine, of Paul. and of Jesus also.

"The advice of Maurice at this point is full of meaning; 'New-Englanders who try to substitute Berkeley or Butler, . . . or Kant or Hegel, for Edwards, and to form their minds upon any of them, must be forcing themselves into an unnatural position, and must suffer from the effort. On the contrary, if they accept the starting point of their native teacher, and seriously consider what is necessary to make that teacher consistent with himself,—what is necessary that the divine foundation upon which he wished to build may not be too weak and narrow for any human or social life to rest upon it,—we should expect great and fruitful results from their inquiries to the land that they must care for most, and therefore to mankind.' The one foundation upon which Edwards wished to build was the absoluteness of God; and he has left for his followers the principle which, if resolutely employed, will ensure both continuity and progress in the thought and life of American Christianity."

The belief of a man or a church contains at least two elements that come to hand, in a measure ready-made,—one is the philosophy of his time, and the other is the general view of history then extant. Possibly there is a third element, which however in one sense is included in philosophy, namely the science of the period. Upon these elements the theologian works. He may indeed modify them, but in so doing he leaves his strictly theological work, which is to combine and interpret philosophy and history, transfusing them with his own religious spirit and his own experience of and from God. The greatest theologians are those who have united, and inspired with religious feeling and insight, philosophy and history. So Paul, Augustine, Aquinas, Calvin and Edwards. The writer believes this is also true of Jesus, despite popular opinion otherwise.

If any person believes those just mentioned or any of them to have been without deep emotion and heart-felt longing and aspiration, if he looks upon them as mere casuits, he shows lack of acquaintance with them. The greatest theologians have united depth of feeling and keenness of insight with a wide view of history as understood in their time. The religious affections of these teachers abide as a permanent good. Their philosophy from time to time, or we might say, constantly, needs correction, amendment, and supplementing, and their history, their world view needs change and enlargement. Progress in theology takes place in this way. It was a favorite simile of Professor Garman's that a dwarf standing on a giant's shoulders could see more than the giant. There is no reason why great credit should be assumed because one can see further than the ones on whom he stands. On the other hand what should be said of one who does not avail himself of the wide range of vision to be thus obtained?

Traditional Christianity has taught that God is absolute, and that Jesus is equal in power, love, and righteousness to God, in fact is God. Philosophy has given a depth of meaning to our thought of God as indwelling spirit, in Whom we have our very being. It teaches that He is absolute and that upon Him we are from moment to moment dependent even for our continued existence.

Turning to history or to historical criticism we find that it teaches that Jesus did not have the power of the eternal God. It upsets the traditional beliefs as to his birth, miracles, resurrection.

The orthodox church shuts its eyes to history. It does not avail itself to the full of the developing philosophy of the time.

The liberal churches for the most part ignore philosophy but accept the results of historical criticism. They say Jesus is not God, and yet continue to worship him, or at least to center all their thought and devotion around him.

The writer feels that it is a great error to speak of the historic Jesus as the second person of the Trinity.

What is lost by abandoning the doctrine of the Trinity, not in the current or historic Unitarian way, which seems to the writer to be for the most part an abandonment of God and an enthronement of the man Jesus, but in order to emphasize the dependence of us all upon the infinite God, who alone is to be perfectly loved, worshipped and adored?

The writer wishes to make his position clear beyond shadow of doubt. He believes Jesus was a man. He believes that God alone is supremely to be loved, trusted and adored, and that our theology and religion should have God as their center, while their circumference should include all the manifestations and works of God. This is not belief in a far-off solitary God. God exists not in three persons, but He is one, yet manifest in infinite multiplicity.

The writer does not believe in the Apostles' Creed. He believes it is sacrilege to worship Jesus. or to pray to him or in his name. He believes in God the Father Almighty, maker of heaven and earth. But Jesus was not his only son. We are all sons of God.

To men in ages past, before the development of modern philosophical conceptions of God, it was harder to worship God alone as Infinite Spirit, and also it was easier to think of Jesus as a metaphysical second person of the Trinity. Today let us rejoice in fuller, larger and more wonderful thought of God. He is the ground of all our life and of all our hopes. Universal religion, centered in belief in one God, Indwelling Spirit, is larger and better, in fact is the fulfillment and completion of traditional Christianity.

"What all religious, poetical, pure, and tender souls are least able to pardon is the diminution or degredation of their ideal. We must never rouse an ideal against us; our business is to point men to another ideal, purer, higher, more spiritual than the old, and so to raise behind a lofty summit one more lofty still. In this way no one is despoiled. . . . Only that which is replaced is destroyed and an ideal is only replaced by satisfying the conditions of the old with some advantages over." Amiel.

Finally, the writer makes his own the words written long, long ago by a Roman Emperor, Marcus Aurelius,— "If any man is able to convince me and show me that I do not think or act right; I will gladly change; for I seek the truth, by which no man was ever injured. But he is injured who abides in his error and ignorance."

CHAPTER VII

A CRITICISM OF MODERN THEOLOGY*

Not in criticism of traditional Christianity, whether that of the Apostles' Creed, of the Roman Church, of Calvinism, or of American Protestant orthodoxy, is the present chapter written. It is assumed that however vigorous these are in outward appearance or however widely held,—it is assumed that these traditional orthodoxies, belong to the past, not the future. So thoroughly have their premises been undermined that these beliefs will fall of themselves as soon as the more progressive churches and schools spread the results of modern study. But does this current liberal theology offer something better? Does it meet deep human need, or give strength to the faint-hearted in life's struggle? Our debt to modern Christian theology, is large,—so much so that it seems ungracious almost for those of us who enter into its heritage to speak the word of criticism. Yet this word needs to be said; and after all will we not better prove ourselves worthy disciples of true scholars and devout men when we transcend their positions than when we accept their conclusions?

Modern Christian theology is essentially negative. It is on the defensive. It is also illogical, but this is the

*Published in practically its present form in *The Open Court* of November 1907.

84

result of its defensive position. Compelled to take away from the old theology continually, its endeavor is to retain the old terms and the old symbols and to show that they have value. There is lacking the all compelling power of a comprehensive gospel that must be preached. The illogical position of modern Christian theology may be seen by a study of its teaching as to the Bible and as to Christ.

1. *The Bible*: Liberal Christianity makes the Bible the great subject of study. True it believes in the composite origin of the Pentateuch, in the Psalms as representing a great number of authors, in the prophetical books as composite, and some, as Daniel, for example, as very late; and one at least, Jonah, as allegorical. It holds even that much of the Old Testament is colored by the prejudices, the fables, and even by the jealousies and hatreds of the Hebrew people. And as for the New Testament, the miraculous element is explained by natural causes or at any rate regarded as the less valuable part of the book. It is said that the part of supreme worth is that which tells us of Christ. Do we ask why the Bible, not being infallible, is taken as the great book of religion, the answer given is that it is by reason of its witness to Christ.

2. *Christ*: Christ is not only the standard by which the Scriptures are judged, but he is the center of theological and religious thought. He is not represented as the metaphysical second person of the Trinity. He is not believed in as the Creator of all things. At least, such expressions as are found in the prologue of John are either interpreted in a figurative sense, or treated simply as a part of the philosophy of that ancient time, which thus

bore witness in its own terms to the moral supremacy
of Jesus. Some believe in the Virgin Birth; some do not.
Many are undecided. Nearly all agree that it is a question of relatively small importance. A few believe in
the bodily, the physical resurrection of Jesus. The majority do not; but believe in what they call the spiritual
resurrection. This teaching concerning Jesus is certainly
far from orthodox. How is it that, Christ is, if anything,
made even more than before the center of theology? It
is said that we find Jesus to be supreme in the realm of
morals and religion.

Modern Liberal theology is Christo-centric because of
what it finds Christ to be. It is Scriptural because the
Bible best teaches us of Christ. And so despite all the
differences between the old theology and the new. the re-
sulting changes in the worship of the churches or in the
statements of religious beliefs are very slight. The
Apostles' Creed can be repeated,—with a moral and
religious rather than a metaphysical interpretation. The
Bible occupies its old time place on the pulpit. Christ is
still the center of religious thought and devotion. And
this theology is professedly based upon the experience of
the church universal.

The theology of a universal religion must be based
upon the experience of the church universal. Notwithstanding its claim it is upon this very point that modern
Christian theology is especially open to criticism. It does
not rest upon universal experience. For one thing it con-
fines itself to the Christian Church. But in the church
of the living God we must include all who in all ages
have been led by the spirit of God. And who have been
thus led? Certainly all who have achieved anything of

goodness or had any visions of new life which they have carried forward to realization; for without God no man can accomplish anything. The experience of Moses and Isaiah surely counts for something; so does the experience of Socrates and Plato, to say nothing of multitudes of true men and women unknown to fame. How contradictory then to appeal to the experience of the church universal to show that all that this church knows of God it knows through Jesus, when great numbers of its members lived before Jesus, and many of those who have come after never even heard of his name! How contradictory,—unless the claim is that even though these patriarchs and leaders and teachers of men, both great and small, did not knowingly receive strength from Christ, yet it was in reality from him that they had power to be and to become sons of God. But the modern theology makes this claim impossible by taking metaphysics from theology and resting its case simply upon the moral supremacy of Jesus. With its denial of a metaphysical Trinity such as our fathers believed in the new theology can no longer speak of Jesus as the light of every man coming into the world. It thus at one sweep, shuts him out from communion with those who lived before he did, and also really denies its own great affirmation that all that the world knows of God it knows from Jesus. But perhaps it is not affirmed so strongly as this that all knowledge of God is through Jesus. Earnest men want the largest and fullest revelation of God it is possible for them to have. · If Christ is not all, why make him the Alpha and Omega of theology and religion?

In reply to all this, perhaps it will be said that the Christian Church by its very existence testifies to the present power of Jesus, or that the individual Christian today does receive strength from him, or that all the best that has been accomplished in the last two thousand years has been done under the influence of Jesus. There is considerable force to such statements. As a great historic person, Jesus has entered into human history and has left an influence that will not cease. Men today are made better when brought under the influence of Jesus. But so also are men made better when brought under the influence of Lincoln, to take a single illustration. And it proves nothing to say that Lincoln influences men for good, because consciously or unconsciously he learned from Jesus, for so also Jesus received from those who lived before his time. Much confusion as to the present power of Jesus in the world today results from lack of clearness on the subject of the resurrection. What is meant by a spiritual resurrection? Is it simply that the apostles thought they saw Jesus? Or is it that his influence has remained on earth? But it is true of all men that the good they do lives after them. Or did Jesus really appear in spiritual form? But if he appeared was it not in bodily form, for who has seen a spirit, or what is a spiritual form?

Then, too, the question of prayer to Jesus or in the name of Jesus is here suggested. Prayer to Jesus if justified at all must be on the ground that Jesus is very God. Men pray only to whom they believe to be a present power. Is Jesus so present: Does he today restrain men from evil? Does he help them be what they ought to be? Yes, he does, but none otherwise than by his example and his influence, as St. Francis does in his own degree. Unless we believe in a metaphysical Christ, who,

like God, or we might say as God, is present, an indwelling
spirit, how can we pray to Jesus?   Modern liberal theology says Christ is not such a spirit, and yet it makes him
the All in All of theology.

Modern theology is at fault in that it does not follow the
logic of its own teachings.   Either the conservatives are
right and the new theology is wrong in its teaching as to
the Bible and Jesus; or, if the new theology is right in
the results of its scholarship, it is open to criticism for
still giving the Bible and Jesus the place it does.   Modern
Christianity has brought the Bible back from its infallible position and given it a place with the world's literature, but it continues to hold it apart from other books.
It has taken the distinctively infinite attributes from Jesus,
it confesses his limitations, yet it worships him and makes
him authoritative;—and why?   Because of his alleged
sinlessness.   But this sinlessness cannot be proven.

We can no more speak of the sinlessness of Jesus than
of the artistic perfection of Michael Angelo or Raphael.
And every one knows that, however great Angelo was as
an artist, he was not perfect.   He lacked some qualities
that Raphael had, and vice versa.   So Jesus lacked some
qualities that Paul had.   To say that by sinlessness, we
mean that Jesus did no wrong,—this is at best a merely
negative statement.   To say that he did everything that
was right and that ought to be done, to say that he combined in perfect degree all good qaulities,—this no man is
able to assert.   If the assertion is made, it is no more valid
than the old proof for the infallibility of the Bible, namely
this,—that when we read it we know that it finds us, and
we are inwardly convinced of the truth of what we read,
hence every word, every part of the Bible, is without error.

It is a similar proof that is offered for the sinlessness of Jesus,—because this or that or all of these incidents reveal his greatness and his goodness, the conclusion is drawn that he was always without fault of any kind. If, however, any one prefers to appeal, as is often done, to the supposition that Jesus, by word or by implication, claimed to be perfect, let such a one remember that a similar proof for the infallibility of the Bible has proven inadequate. Unless Jesus perfectly and completely reveals all of God that we know, why make him the one leader, the one teacher, the one example? No man, not even Jesus, is great enough, or wise enough, or good enough, to be the sole authority in morals and religion.

Modern theology fails to meet the universal need not simply by reason of what it teaches, but far more by reason of what it neglects to say. It is at fault in confining itself to the Bible not so much because the Bible is not helpful as because there are other messages from God. To take one illustration, God spoke to the ancient Greeks in a way that He did not speak to the Hebrews or to any one else; and the Christian Church by taking no account of this message in neglecting the Word of God. To be sure, the Christian Church does not forbid men to study or to read these words spoken to other peoples than the Hebrews, but it does not, as a religion ought to do, stop men in the busy rush of life and say,—hold, here is a word of God to you. It does not in church or church school tell of that real Word of God, which comprises all the great truths which courageous souls have seized upon down through the entire stream of human life. And God has sent us prophets even in recent years. There are Victor Hugo, and Goethe, and Browning and Tennyson, and Carlyle with his message that might is divine because the only power that can accomplish lasting results is power that is righteous; and there is Emerson to teach us that self-reliance which is trust in the Spirit within and above us. And there is Abraham Lincoln. As many lessons are to be gained by study of his life as that of David, who was taken from tending his father's sheep and made ruler over Israel. It is not enough once a year to suspend, as it were, religious exercises and preach a patriotic sermon on Washington or Lincoln, or of an evening discuss the poetry of Browning or Tennyson. There is need of clear and emphatic witness to the great fact that the all-comprehending God has given us the enduring literature of all nations as part of His Divine Word. And this Word asks not toleration, but demands its rightful place as the Book of the Church.

And modern theology fails in confining itself so much to the historic Jesus, not because his teaching is not helpful or his life inspiring, but because the Eternal Father, the Ever-present Spirit is the one for whom our souls hunger and thirst. And He has not confined the revelation of Himself to one age or to one man. The Father Almighty spoke to Moses, He made Caesar the instrument of His will, He gave Paul zeal for the gospel he had experienced. He was the Father of Jesus, and the God of Aquinas. He came to Mohammed in Arabia. He inspired Gautama with pity. Yes, and God is in the world today, the all real, the all vital, the all conquering fact of life. No mother's love but is token of a fuller love of God; no father's care but is from Him.

Did we think of saying that the Bible and Jesus adequately and perfectly reveal God? Millenniums of years and countless lives have told us only a little of His greatness and His goodness. Modern Christianity fails because it points men backward rather than forward for the ideal. The best is yet to be. Universal religion demands a universal Bible and an ever present God. Unless modern Christianity succeeds in showing the Bible, as at present constituted, to be absolutely unique, there must be a revision of the canon. Those who chose the present one are not competent to bind us today, any more than Ezra was competent to select the Gospels or the other New Testament books. How could he be when he lived before they were written? Unless modern Christianity can show as it has not yet done that Jesus, the historic man of Nazareth, is to be identified in a unique way with the ever present Spirit of God, it must cease to center around him. And it is not enough to appeal to the experience of the great body of Christians, for it stands to reason that even as one who had never traveled beyond his native country, nor even read of foreign lands, unless with the object of becoming more firmly convinced of his own country's pre-eminence, even as such a one would believe all the good to be within his own fatherland and base his claim perhaps upon his own experience, so those who confine their religious reading to the Bible or books about the Bible, and their thought of God to Jesus, as the great body of Christians has done, would regard this book as pre-eminently the Word of God and Jesus the one authority, and, to prove these things, quote from their own experience. Nor can the burden of proof be shifted. It does not rest with such as the writer, but with modern Christians, because they are the ones who have themselves denied the infallibility of the Bible and the deity of Jesus.

It lies before them either to present some valid reason for not accepting the logic of their own results, or else, accepting it, to pass from Christianity to universal religion.

CHAPTER VIII

AFFIRMATIVE THEOLOGY*

Changes in theology have been so fundamental that to-day there must be a large amount of destructive work done. The end has not been reached by Biblical criticism. It is in theology itself that discussion is needed. A previous chapter entitled "A Criticism of Modern Theology" was mainly negative in tone, a denial of the prevailing theology of the present. No man loves scepticism. Doubt does not nerve us for action. Let a positive statement follow the criticism. But especially let it be emphasized over and over again, that before we can build upon the solid rock, all the imaginary, the unreal, the merely traditional, must be swept away. The positive statement that follows comes not before, but after rejection of Jesus, the Bible and the name of Christian, as these are commonly accepted even by liberals.

Without further preliminary I state my own theology. Where shall we start? Where must I start except with myself? *I am thinking,* said Descartes, and this has become the starting point of modern philosophy. I know myself as thinking, feeling, willing,—but I have through it all a feeling of absolute dependence. I need no argument to prove it. Dependent upon what? Upon whom? Here does religion begin,—in our every breath we are dependent. Upon what, upon whom? Upon something

*Published in practically its present form in *The Open Court* July 1908.

within and yet not ourselves. This something, this Spirit. I will call God. The fact of dependence is an ultimate fact. The nature of the spirit upon whom we are dependent is, however, open to long discussion.

In my daily life I have to do with persons and with things—they are external—they are outside of me. But they cannot be entirely foreign to me else I could not know them. Recall your epistemology; what is your theory of knowledge? The objective becomes known to us only as we make it subjective. But how can the objective become subjective? And surely to be known it must so become,—unless all is more subjectively, anyway, no external reality at all.

This is a chapter on theology, hence I pass over these philosophical questions with the briefest discussion possible. The objective can become subjective only because it is already and always subjective to that power, that spirit, upon whom we depend. So we go out of ourselves and find that which is deepest within us—scientific form of the old truth,—*He that loseth his life saveth it.* Would you be wiser than all, keep your knowledge to yourself; would you be richer than all, bury your gold; would you be stronger than all, waste not your energy; we all know the folly of such advice. Rather, if you would know a science, or a language, teach it to somebody else; would you increase in wealth, ever spend in investment; the athlete becomes such through fatigue and wearisome exercise. Would you know yourself, know others, study their thoughts and words and works. But all the objective must be made subjective, else the result is no more beneficial than unassimilated, undigested food. The faith of Jesus must be no longer his faith but our faith, the zeal of Paul must become our zeal; the equanimity of Socrates likewise must become yours and mine; the struggles of Augustine and his rest found in God, if they remain foreign to us, help us not.

Let us look back over the way thus far traveled. The primary fact with us all is that *we are*, and it is *dependent* that *we are*. Constantly we are reaching out of ourselves to external objects and persons which we mysteriously grasp and make our own. This we are able to do because that something, that power, that spirit upon which we are dependent is that upon which they also are dependent. Thus, that which is objective to us we can yet make subjective because it is subjective to that spirit within and above us upon whom we depend. Unless this is so our knowledge is no knowledge. The fact of dependence is the primary fact of life. In our hours of solitude and meditation we are aware of a spirit not our own; in our hours of busiest life it is still upon a spirit not ourselves that we are dependent.

Since we are all dependent upon a spirit not ourselves, absolutely dependent, it is the important question of life (to say nothing of its being fundamental in theology) what is and what ought to be our relation to that power. The question of God is first and last and always the all important one. Every one must agree upon this. Those who say we can know nothing about him, those who say he lived once in human form in Galilee, and those who give any other answer whatsoever, must all agree that the question is of primary importance. If this is so it seems strange indeed that any who do not believe that Jesus was God should put the proclamation of the faith of that man as the great mission of the church today. To me it seems like giving the hungering soul a stone. He comes asking for God and he is given a man. He comes saying, "Show me the Father". We show him Jesus and say, This is not the Father, but let it suffice you.

God: What do we know about God?—This is the question. Even as I know myself as dependent and grasping objects with the embrace of my consciousness, so I know with all the assurance with which I know anything at all, that there is a Being upon whom I am dependent and who is everywhere the ground and source of all my universe. And how much needed is emphasis upon this fact today—for it is a fact, not a conjecture. Liberal churches have little power because they have lost the sense of the reality of God; they make the Fatherhood of God merely a background for the Brotherhood of man; and the old time theology has whatever power it has, not because of its unscientific notions and many errors, but because it has not lost the perspective and put man first, God second.

Recurring to our question, What do we know about God?—this is to be answered largely by asking another question, Where do we learn of God? We learn of God at first hand by actual experience and relation with Him. In all our lives we are constantly meeting that Spirit upon whom we depend. Hence our knowledge of God differs one from another as our experience differs; the larger the experience, the larger the knowledge. This is why we ought to know more about God today than Jesus did. It must, however, be borne in mind that only as we assimilate knowledge does it become our own. It is true, then, that in a very real sense every man has his own God. But we are able without fear of contradiction to maintain the unity of God and that this God who is one is eternal, omnipresent, omniscient and omnipotent.

From the unity of our own self-conscious life, we are forced to believe in the unity of that Spirit upon whom we depend. If God is not one, there is more than one universe. No man knows more than one.

Eternity is unity of time. Apart from God no time exists.

Omnipresence is unity of space—there is no place where God is not.

Omniscience is unity of knowledge. We know objects not immediately but mediately. God's knowledge is immediate,—that of self-consciousness. We know immediately only in the present, here and now. With such immediacy does God know all things in all time and in all places.

Omnipotence is unity of power. God is the source of law. There is for him no external authority. All God's law is self-imposed law.

Thus far we have taken only the preliminary steps. I would emphasize again and again, however, that this is not theory but reality;—that I can be sure and do know with all positiveness, not as faith but as knowledge, that there is a power, a spirit, one in time, space, knowledge and power. in whom my life is grounded and in whose universe I live. Upon this power I am absolutely dependent.

Turning again to my own experience, I find moral attributes which I would ascribe to this power. Such are justice, righteousness, holiness, mercy, love, and every other virtue. But how about intemperance. anger. lust, malice, envy and all the vices? The problem of evil in our own lives and in the world confronts us. We are not able with the same assurance as before to ascribe the moral attributes to God, i.e., not as a matter of knowledge. The problem of evil from a philosophical standpoint is among the most difficult of problems. No attempt at its discussion is here made. I simply state my own belief. I believe in the perfect justice and righteousness and purity and mercy and love of that Spirit whom henceforth we call God. This is a belief not without grounds; in myself I find these qualities and in others I see them, but never in their perfection. Yet whence comes the ideal. Its presence carries a certain weight of evidence as to its reality. I could not from myself get the ideal of perfection, for I do not find perfection there, or in the world about me.

Salvation: Every theology must meet the test of human need. It must answer that ever recurring question of which the old form was "What must I do to be saved?" We put it, Where and how can we get salvation, i.e., How can we become what we ought to be? Some say salvation is by character, an absurd statement,—as absurd as it would be if I should answer some poor, wandering, lost child who asked me how he could find the way home, "You can get there by being there." Saved by character, —but how get a good character when we have a bad one? Again is God left out of account. It is assumed that we of ourselves can become true and holy. The fact is we are always saved by the grace of God. What do we mean by this? The ideal is from God. It is not from ourselves that we have a desire for a better life or that we behold the vision of what we ought to be. Whatever be the secondary means of grace, the ultimate source is God. From

Him we receive not only the ideal but strength to attain it. The standing miracle of the ages is the fact of an inexhaustible supply of power. We can have what we will take, as our faith so is the gift. Psychology and theology alike teach salvation by faith.

Evolution must be reckoned with in all our thinking, but Darwinian and moral evolution are as far removed as the East from the West. In Darwinian evolution, there is struggle for existence, the weak perish, the strong survive through the death of the weak. Progress is exceedingly slow; only through long ages does a slight advance take place. In moral evolution, there is struggle, not for existence, but struggle for righteousness; the weak survive, being made strong out of weakness; if any perish, it is the strong for the weak; progress may be exceedingly rapid. What is the religious struggle but for righteousness? All history tells us of this struggle; its pages are filled with tales of heroes, of cowards made valiant; the martyr rolls are covered with the names of the strong who died for the weak, and that progress may be rapid needs no argument. A man who is traveling east needs scarcely a second in which to wheel about westward. In as little time may a sinner turn from evil to good. There can be no denial of this.

Prayer: Belief in God and belief in prayer go hand in hand. In harmony with the theology thus far outlined in this chapter, there are three distinct elements to be noted in prayer.

1. We do pray—every deep desire finds expression in some form of prayer when we are thoroughly conscious of the presence of God pervading our life. The relation between ourselves and God is so close, so literally and

actually do we live, move and have our being in Him that our every ardent wish for better things does come as a true prayer. Thus we pray for strength to withstand temptation, for wisdom. for the coming of His Kingdom. But to every such prayer, we seem always to hear the answer, *I have given you strength, work out your own salvation.* And so

2. To labor is to pray. To meet every circumstance and event of life as it comes and to do our best, constantly and reverently seeking to be guided by all our experience, is to trust God and to follow the guidance of Him from whom all events come. To do our best in dependence upon God is as truly prayer as is the expression of the lip or the secret whisper of the heart. The religious man, the one who believes in the perfection of God and who dares to live in such belief and trust, lives a life of prayer. He is conscious of his continuous need of God, and to Him his soul ever reaches out. And so

3. We must ever come back to our dependence upon God and in prayer, acknowledge that whatever be our striving, we cannot of ourselves answer our prayer or govern the results of our efforts—but our helpless souls do depend on Him.

Take an illustration to explain this threefold aspect of prayer. . We pray for strength to do the right and to be what God means us to be, "to be saved" as the old phrase has it. The answer seems ever to come, Why are you kneeling here before me? Rise and be the man that you ought to be, do the right, answer your own prayer, and so we commence to pray by living, but do we accomplish anything by our own strength? It is God alone that must bless our striving. He, and He alone, must save.

God's Word: The nurture of the religious life is naturally suggested by the subject of prayer. Aside from prayer, which is communion with God within, there is reading of God's Word and fellowship with the people of God. Needless to say, by Word of God we do not mean the Bible of the Christian. We mean all the deepest and best, all the enduring of the world's literature. Liberals who raise aloft the Christian Bible as the one book never tire of speaking of it as the literature of the Hebrew people. Yes, answer those who stand with me, but we are heirs of all the ages, we are citizens of the world, none less than the enduring literature of the world shall be our Bible. To speak of such as "God's Word," is no figure of speech, nor will we hesitate to stand by our belief in its divine inspiration.

Holy men of old spake as they were moved by the Holy Ghost, says the Christian. We say likewise. But to be moved by the Holy Ghost is not something so unusual or unnatural as has been supposed. The Holy Ghost is God, the Indwelling Spirit. He speaks to all who listen. He speaks through all our experience. Those who have had the largest and best experience of God, who have sought and found him, they have spoken as they were moved by the Spirit of God. Every true word, every enduring message is divinely inspired. The canon of our Scriptures is never closed, for to close the canon is to shut the gate of our temple to God Himself.

Let no man reproach me with taking away any man's Bible. Those who stand with me are the ones who ought to rise up in strength and to Christians say, You shall not take from us God's Word and hand us in lieu thereof a closed book, a few letters and sermons, some history, a few hymns and proverbs. We will not be content with less than all we can use. The test of the canon is that which endures, endures by finding an answer in the lives of those who read. God, speaking through others, finds an answer in God within. Our religious life can attain its fullness only by constant use of God's Word. Here we have spread out before us the results of the whole world's experience and knowledge of God. All is ready for us, but to make it really our own we must live it over, learning from their mistakes and successes alike, completing and filling up their knowledge of God.

Church Fellowship: But for the best results, the religious life must also be nurtured by fellowship with those of like aims and purposes. Hence churches, their place and necessity.

Needless to argue upon this point. But a few observations are not out of place as to the bond of union. Shall it be creed or a covenant, or what shall it be? Certainly a church ought not to be select or restrictive, it then becomes a club or society, not a church. The true church is all-embracing, comprehensive, and would have none outside. Surely no creed ought to be such as will bar a man out.

The charge against Christianity is twofold, that it rests upon unreality, the deity of Jesus, and that consequently it is exclusive. Such theology as I have been insistent upon takes reality for its corner stone,—not intellectual truth but the very nature of things. Hence it asks not for acceptance of any name or uniform, any symbol or book. It seeks not to enforce or persuade unity, but to declare and make known what is. The Christian missionary would carry to the ends of the earth his Jesus and ask allegiance and surrender to him. Very different is the course I would pursue. And surely, surely, we should be for this reason the more zealous, the more large-minded, the more farseeking—but it is not to bring others to allegiance to any man of some particular time or place in history, but first of all to bring to their attention the fact of their relation to God, and as already repeated, the doctrine of God rests not upon conjecture but upon reality. Then the appeal is for faith, not about matters of fact or content of knowledge, but faith in choice.

The common creed of the church universal, may it more and more clearly become none else than in substance this: I believe in the perfect righteousness and justice and holiness and mercy and wisdom and love of God, and I dare to accept this belief with my whole heart and soul and make the supreme choice of God for my Saviour and my King, for my Friend above all friends.

The Chinaman can accept this without ever having heard of Palestine. At the same time it is a duty and privilege of the strong in faith and rich in opportunity to freely give as they have freely received. All things are ours; to attain the largest life we must receive from all humanity the results of its life and experience.

Conversion: Our favored land has peculiar responsibility for the conversion of the world, but we have also much to learn from those whom the Christian calls the heathen. I used the word conversion. Explanation is needed. By it I mean conscious acceptance of a perfect God for our Saviour. He is our Father, our King, our Friend. We are already members of His Household, and His Kingdom; we are, everybody is, dwelling under His care and living by His grace. We need no adoption of sonship, but only to accept His Fatherhood.

Atonement: Finally the expression of the religious life is loving service in bringing the world to God through fellowship with Him in His redemptive work. I dare to believe and live in the belief that God is perfect. He then sorrows in all our sorrows, suffers in all our suffering, and ever seeks to bring the world to Himself through His at-one-ment of love and mercy which does make us to know His goodness and His greatness and fills us with desire to be like Himself, and He helps us so to become. The life of faith means, then, not a life of ease or of pleasure, but of heroic, earnest, never ending giving of self.

Immortality: One question which is usually dealt with in theology is thus far omitted here, namely that of immortality. What can we hope for? Needless to say Christian eschatology is discredited, yet the human heart does desire the strength and comfort of Heaven. The future, however, must remain among things hoped for—it belongs to faith, not to knowledge. It is not to be used as a motive for conversion or an incentive to righteousness. Righteousness must be demanded on its own ground, for its own sake. The one reason why we should seek salvation, is that we may be like God, be what we ought to be, and that, regardless of the future or the present.

The question of immortality, after all, does not primarily concern us. To be right with God is our concern. The question of immortality is thus to be brought into relation with our belief in God. I dare to believe in the perfection of God. I may think this implies immortality, or, again, there may be grounds for doubting it. I certainly am able to form no adequate or satisfactory con-

ception of another life, but what of that? My concern is
that I may ever rest in God and trust Him at all times.
To Him there is no past, no future, but an eternal present.
To Him I give my life. To know Him and have fellowship with Him is for me life eternal. It is all of life.
God is the Lord of life. Belief in immortality must be
based not upon legends of the past, but upon belief in a
perfect God.

Concluding Remarks: The writer offers no apology
for leaving the beaten track of theological discussion.
Theology will one day again be queen of the sciences, its
rightful place, for when we center our thought where our
experience is centered, in God, then all science, all life
becomes sacred. The astronomer is not studying the
work of another than God. Any conflict between science
and theology is absurd. True theology uses the results
of the various sciences, it inspires them, it synthesizes
and interprets their fragmentary and scattered results in
their relation to life.

One word more by way of final summary. The orthodox Christian identifies God and the historic Jesus of
Nazareth. This identification is becoming every day
more impossible intellectually, and practically also. Surely such identification is a great error. There is no identity
in reality. Either one of two courses may be taken by
those who agree that such identity is absolutely dis-
proven. God and Jesus are not the same. The liberals
generally agree with this. They say this is so, we hold
to Jesus, he shall be central, to proclaim his faith is our
task. My whole criticism summed up in a word is against
the supreme choice of Jesus and the forgetting of God.
As for me, I choose God.

CHAPTER IX

RELIGIOUS WRITINGS

Several times in this little book, statement has been made to the effect that the Bible does not contain all of the Word of God. More especially in the two preceding chapters has it been emphasized that objection to the Bible as the one authoritative Word of God rests both upon denial of its infallible authority, and even more, than upon what is included, upon what is not contained therein. We do well in no uncertain terms to deny the orthodox position as to the Scriptures. But it is even more important to emphasize that God's Word includes much that is not contained within the covers of the Bible.

In this chapter we pass over for the time being, or rather defer to a subsequent section of this book, the need and necessity for correlating and bringing together, in our religious thought and teaching, all phases of life, including science, government, business, ethics, and aesthetics, as well as the more distinctively religious.

The modern liberal Christian emphasizes the Bible as a book of religious inspiration, and upon this ground seeks to establish for it a position as unique and distinctive, as even under the older theory of its infallibility.

It would be easy to point out that some parts of the Bible have no distinctive religious teaching. For example what religious teaching or element of inspiration is in passages such as the genealogical tables in the first part of First Chronicles or in other verses which could be picked out readily by any one familiar with the Bible.

But even so, even if there are some passages without religious but only of historic or antiquarian value, this does not detract from the more valuable parts, the familiar passages which have been so treasured in religious experience, and have become a priceless heritage. Rather than attempt to criticize passages of little or of doubtful value, let us devote our attention to the loss that we suffer not from religious treasuring of Biblical passages, but from failure to recognize as of equal worth passages of religious teaching and inspiration from non-Biblical sources. Of course if the Bible is infallible and alone has that degree of authority, passages from other literature are not to be compared with it. But if, as is so common at present, the appeal is to religious and inspirational value, let us be fair and consider whether the Bible is so unique as has been claimed, ostensibly upon the ground of religious value, but in reality upon inherited ideas as to authority.

It is not claimed that all of these passages, or necessarily that any of them are better than some quotations from the Bible,—but it is claimed that they surpass some parts of the Bible and equal other parts, in religious value today, and that church services and Sunday schools, as well as individual devotional reading and study, would be benefited by a wider range and a more inclusive use of literature.

The following quotations are illustrative only and have been selected at random. Names of writers are not mentioned because of our desire to have the attention center upon the quotations rather than upon their sources. The writers cover a wide range of time, space, and experience, and are both from within and outside of the Christian tradition.

"Do not despise your situation,—in it you must act, suffer, and conquer. From every point on earth we are equally near to heaven and to the infinite."

"Heaven and earth may pass away, but good ought to be, and injustice ought not to be. Such is the creed of the human race. Nature will be conquered by spirit; the eternal will triumph over time."

"The germ of all things are in every heart, and the greatest criminals as well as the greatest heroes are but different modes of ourselves. Only evil grows of itself, while for goodness we want effort and courage."

"How sure it is,
That, if we say a true word, instantly
We feel 'tis God's, not ours, and pass it on,
Like bread at sacrament we taste and pass,
Nor handle for a moment, as indeed
We dared to set up any claim to such!"

"Spiritual pride commonly occasions a certain stiffness and inflexibility in persons, in their own judgment and their own way, whereas the eminently humble person, though he is inflexible in his duty, and in those things wherein God's honor is concerned; and with regard to temptation to those things he apprehends to be sinful, though in never so small a degree. he is not at all of a yieldable spirit, but is like a brazen wall; yet in other things he is of a pliable disposition, not disposed to set up his own opinion or his own will,—he is ready to pay deference to others' opinions, and loves to comply with their inclinations and has a heart that is tender and flexible like a little child."

"No iron chain, or outward force of any kind, could ever compel the soul of man to believe or to disbelieve: It is his own indefeasible light, that judgment of his: he will reign, and believe there, by the grace of God alone."

"The Maker's Laws, whether they are promulgated in Sinai Thunder, to the ear or imagination, or quite otherwise promulgated, are the Laws of God; transcendent, imperatively demanding obedience from all men. This, without any thunder, thou, if there be any soul left in thee, canst know of a truth. The Universe is made by Law; the great Soul of the world is just and not unjust."

"It is written, 'Many shall run to and fro, and knowledge shall be increased.' Surely the plain rule is, Let each considerate person have his way, and see what it will lead to. For not this man and that man, but all men make up mankind, and their united tasks the task of mankind. How often have we seen some such adventurous, and perhaps much-censured wanderer light on some outlying, neglected, yet vitally momentous province: the hidden treasure of which he first discovered, and kept proclaiming till the general eye and effort were directed thither, and the conquest was completed;—thereby, in these his seemingly so aimless rambles, planting new standards, founding new habitable colonies, in the im-

measurable circumambient realm of Nothingness and
Night! Wise man was he who counseled that Speculation should have free course, and look fearlessly towards
all the thirty-two points of the compass, whithersoever
and howsoever it listed."

> "Wisely, my son, while yet thy days are long,
> And this fair change of seasons passes slow,
> Gather and treasure up the good they yield—
> All that they teach of virtue, of pure thoughts
> And kind affections, reverence for thy God
> And for thy brethren; so, when thou shalt come
> Into these barren years, thou mayst not bring
> A mind unfurnished and a withered heart."

"O most merciful God, grant to me Thy grace, that it
may be with me, and work with me, and continue with me
even to the end.

"Grant that I may always desire and will that which is
to Thee most acceptable and most dear.

Let Thy will be mine, and let my will ever follow
Thine, and agree perfectly with it.

Grant to me above all things that I can desire, to de-
sire to rest in Thee, and in Thee to have my heart at peace.
Thou art the true peace of the heart; Thou art its only
rest; out of Thee all things are full of trouble and unrest.
In this peace, that is, in Thee, the one chiefest eternal
Good, I will lay me down and sleep. Amen."

"But so much more malignant and more savage
Becomes the land untilled and with bad seed
The more good earthly vigor it possesses."

"Whatsoever hath the Church in keeping
Is for the folk that ask it in God's Name."

"For who repents not cannot be absolved,
Nor can one both repent and will at once,
Because of the contradiction which consents not."

"Horrible my iniquities had been;
But Infinite Goodness hath such ample arms,
That it receives whatever turns to it."

"A man may use as much art as he likes in order to
paint to himself an unlawful act that he remembers, as an
unintentional error, a mere oversight. such as one can
never altogether avoid, and therefore as something in
which he was carried away by the stream of physical
necessity, and thus to make himself out innocent, yet he
finds that the advocate who speaks in his favour can by
no means silence the accuser within, if only he is conscious
that at the time when he did this wrong he was in his
senses, that is, in possession of his freedom."

"Hear the just law—judgment of the skies!
He that hates the truth shall be the dupe of lies;
And he that will be cheated to the last,
Delusions strong as hell shall bind him fast."

"Thou art the source and centre of all minds,
Their only point of rest, eternal Word!
From Thee departing, they are lost and rove
At random without honour. hope or peace.
From Thee is all that soothes the life of man,

His high endeavor, and his glad success,
His strength to suffer, and his will to serve.
But, O Thou bounteous giver of all good,
Thou art of all Thy gifts the crown!
Give what Thou canst, without Thee we are poor;
And with Thee, rich, take what Thou wilt away."

"Two things fill the mind with ever new and increasing admiration and awe, the oftener and the more steadily we reflect on them: *the starry heavens above and the moral law within.* I have not to search for them and conjecture them as though they were veiled in darkness or were in the transcendent region beyond my horizon; I see them before me and connect them directly with the consciousness of my existence. The former begins from the place I occupy in the external world of sense, and enlarges my connection therein to an unbounded extent with worlds upon worlds and systems of systems, and moreover into limitless times of their periodic motion, its beginning and continuance. The second begins from my invisible self, my personality, and exhibits me in a world which has true infinity, but which is traceable only by the understanding, and with which I discern that I am not in a merely contingent but in a universal and necessary connexion, as I am also thereby with all those visible worlds. The former view of a countless multitude of worlds annihilates, as it were, my importance as an *animal creature*, which after it has been for a short time provided with vital power, one knows not how, must again give back the matter of which it was formed to the planet it inhabits (a mere speck in the universe). The second, on the contrary, infinitely elevates my worth as an *in-*

telligence by my personality, in which the moral law reveals to me a life independent on animality and even on the whole sensible world—at least so far as may be inferred from the destination assigned to my existence by this law, a destination not restricted to conditions and limits of this life, but reaching into the infinite."

"Above all things, and in all things, my soul, thou shalt rest in the Lord always, for He Himself is the everlasting rest of the saints.

Grant me to rest in Thee, above all creatures, above all health and beauty, above all glory and honor, above all power and dignity, above all knowledge and subtlety, above all riches and arts, above all joy and gladness, above all fame and praise, above all sweetness and comfort, above all hope and promise, above all desert and desire; above all gifts and benefits that Thou canst give and impart unto us, above all mirth and joy that the mind of man can receive and feel; above all that Thou art not, O my God."

"The law of the soul, which we call reason, reigns with an absolute sway; its reproaches are ever uttered and repeated at what is wrong; it sets bounds to the folly of the most audacious.

After vice has enjoyed so many ages of unrestrained sway, virtue is still called virtue; and it cannot be dispossessed of its name by its boldest and most brutal enemies. From thence it is that vice, although triumphant in the world, is still forced to disguise itself under the mask of hypocrisy, that it may secure a regard that it does not hope for when it is known as it is. Thus it renders in spite of itself, homage to virtue, by adorning itself with her charms, that it may receive the honors that are rendered to them. Men cavil, it is true, at the virtuous, and they are in truth, always liable to censure, for they are still imperfect; but the most vicious men cannot succeed in effacing entirely the idea of virtue. No man has ever succeeded in persuading others or himself, that it is more estimable to be deceitful than to be sincere; to be violent and malignant than to be gentle and do good. This inward and universal teacher declares the same truths, at all times and places. It is true that we often contradict it, and speak with a louder voice; but then we deceive ourselves, we go astray, we fear that we shall discover that we are wrong, and we shut our ears, lest we should be humbled by its corrections. Where is this wisdom, where is this oracle that ever speaks, and against which the prejudices of mankind can never prevail? Where is this noble reason that we are bound to consult, and which of itself inspires us with a desire to hear its voice? Where dwells this pure and gentle light, that not only enlightens eyes that are open to receive it, but uncloses those eyes that are shut, cures those that were diseased, gives vision to the blind; in short, inspires a desire for the light it can bestow, and makes itself beloved even by those who fear it?

Every eye has it; it is by its pure rays alone that it can see anything. As the visible sun enlightens all material bodies, so the sun of intelligence illuminates all minds.

There is a spiritual sun that enlightens the soul more fully than the material sun does the body. This sun of truth leaves no shadow, and it shines upon both hemispheres. It is as brilliant in the night as in the day time:

it is not without that it sheds its rays, it dwells within each of us. One man cannot hide its rays from another; whatever corner of the earth we go to, there it is. We never need say to another, Stand back that I may see it; you hide its rays from me; you deprive me of the portion that is my due. This glorious sun never sets; no clouds intercept its rays, but those formed by our passions. It is one bright day. It sheds light upon the savage in the darkest caverns. There are no eyes so weak that they cannot bear its light; and there is no man so blind and miserable, that does not walk by the feeble light from this source, that he still retains in his conscience.

We believe the instructions of men just in proportion to the conformity we find between them and this inward teacher. After they have exhausted all their reasonings, we still return to this, and listen to the decision it makes. If anyone tells me that a part is equal to the whole, I cannot help laughing; such a one, cannot persuade me: it is within myself by consulting this inward teacher, that I must ascertain the truth of a proposition.

Far from pronouncing judgment upon this teacher, we are in all cases judged by it. It is disinterested and superior to us. We may refuse to listen to it, and go astray from it; but if we do listen, we cannot contradict it. There seem to be two kinds of reason within me; one is self, the other superior to it. That which is self, is very imperfect; prejudiced, rash, apt to wander, changing, obstinate, ignorant, and limited; it possesses nothing that is not borrowed. The other, while it is common to all men, is yet superior to them; it is perfect, eternal, immutable, always ready to be communicated, and to reclaim the erring;—given freely to all, inexhaustible, and indivisible. Where is this all perfect reason so near me, yet so different from me? Where is it? Where dwells this supreme reason? Is it not God Himself?"

> "But fresh and green from the rotting roots
> Of primal forests the young growth shoots;
> From the death of the old the new proceeds,
> And the life of truth from the rot of creeds:
> On the ladder of God, which upwards leads,
> The steps of progress are human needs.
> For His Judgments still are a mighty deep,
> And the eyes of His providence never sleep:
> When the night is darkest He gives the morn:
> When the famine is sorest, the wine and corn!"

"For not by the movement of our feet, and not by spaces that can be measured, do we fly from Thee or return to Thee? Did that younger son of Thine hire horses or chariot or ship, did he fly on real wings, or walk with real legs to that far off land where he spent in riotous living all that Thou gavest at his setting forth? In love Thou gavest O Father; in greater love Thou forgavest the returning prodigal. A lustful heart is that far off land, a land of darkness, far from Thy face."

"The common problem, yours, mine, every one's,
Is—not to fancy what were fair in life
Provided it could be,—but, finding first
What may be, then find how to make it fair."

"God's gift was that man should conceive of truth
And yearn to gain it, catching at mistakes,
As midway help till he reach fact indeed.

The statuary ere he mold a shape
Boasts a like gift, the shape's idea, and next
The aspiration to produce the same;
So taking clay, he calls his shape thereout;
Cries ever 'Now I have the thing I see:'
Yet all the while goes changing what was wrought,
From falsehood like the truth, to truth itself."

"The beautiful is as useful as the useful. Perhaps more
    so."

"Thou who art!
Ecclesiastes names Thee the Almighty; Maccabees
names Thee Creator; the Epistle to the Ephesians names
Thee Liberty; Baruch names Thee Immensity; the Psalms
name Thee Wisdom and Truth; John names Thee Light;
the Books of Kings name Thee Lord; Exodus calls Thee
Providence; Leviticus, Holiness; Esdras, Justice; Crea-
tion calls Thee God; man names Thee Father; but Sol-
omon names Thee Compassion, and that is the most beautiful of all Thy names."

"Man lives by affirmation even more than he does by
bread."

"There is no backward flow of ideas more than of
rivers.
But let those who desire not the future think of it. In
saying no to progress it is not the future which they condemn, but themselves. They give themselves a melan-
choly disease; they inoculate themselves with the past.
There is but one way of refusing tomorrow, that is to die.
Now. no death, that of the body as late as possible,
that of the soul, never, is what we desire."

"Be not ashamed to be helped; for it is thy business to do thy duty like a soldier in the assault on a town. How, then, if being lame thou canst not mount up on the battlements alone, but with the help of another it is possible?"

"When God makes His presence felt through us, we are like the burning bush; Moses never took any heed what sort of a bush it was—he only saw the brightness of the Lord."

"There is no despair so absolute as that which comes with the first moments of our first great sorrow, when we have not yet known what it is to have suffered and be healed, to have despaired and to have recovered hope."

"The great river-courses which have shaped the lives of men have hardly changed; and those other streams, the life-currents that ebb and flow in human hearts, pulsate to the same great needs, the same great loves and terrors. As our thought follows close to the slow wake of the dawn. we are impressed with the broad sameness of the human lot, which never alters in the main headings of its history—hunger and labor, seed-time and harvest, love and death."

"These things have not changed. The sunlight and shadows bring their old beauty and waken the old heart strains at morning, noon, and eventide; the little children are still the symbol of the eternal marriage between love and duty; and men still yearn for the reign of peace and righteousness—still own that life to be the highest which is a conscious voluntary sacrifice."

"It is only a poor sort of happiness that could ever come by caring very much about our own narrow pleasures. We can only have the highest happiness, such as goes along with being a great man, by having wide thoughts, and much feeling for the rest of the world, as well as ourselves; and this sort of happiness often brings so much pain with it, that we can only tell it from pain by its being what we would choose before everything else, because our souls see it is good. There are so many things wrong and difficult in the world, that no man can be great —he can hardly keep himself from wickedness—unless he gives up thinking much about pleasures or rewards, and gets strength to endure what is hard and painful.

*   *   *   *   *   *

There was a man to whom I was very near, so that I could see a great deal of his life, who made almost every one fond of him, for he was young and clever, and beautiful, and his manners to all were gentle and kind. I believe when I first knew him, he never thought of anything cruel or base. But because he tried to slip away from everything that was unpleasant, and cared for nothing else so much as his own safety, he came at last to commit some of the basest deeds—such as make men infamous. He denied his father, and left him to misery; he betrayed every trust that was reposed in him, that he might keep himself safe and get rich and prosperous. Yet calamity overtook him."

"An ancient land in ancient oracles
Is called 'law-thirsty'; all the struggle there
Was after order and a perfect rule.
Pray where lie such lands now?

Why, where they lay of old—in human souls."

"Even as in a sea voyage, when the ship is brought to anchor and you go out to fetch in water, you make a by-work of gathering a few roots and shells by the way, but have need ever to keep your mind fixed on the ship, and constantly to look around, lest at any time the master of the ship call, and you must, if he call, cast away all those things, lest you be treated like the sheep that are bound and thrown into the hold: So it is with human life."

"It is the part of the stranger and alien in God's world who fights against God in the one way he can—by his own opinions."

"Concerning the Gods, there are some who say that a divine being does not exist; and, others, that it exists indeed, but it is idle and uncaring, and hath no forethought for anything; and a third class say that there is such a Being, and he taketh forethought also, but only in respect of great and heavenly things but of nothing that is on the earth; and a fourth class, that he taketh thought both of things in heaven and earth, but only in general, and not of each thing severally. And there is a fifth class . . . who say, *Nor Can I move Without Thy Knowledge.*"

"O Lord, how entirely needful is Thy grace for me, to begin any good work, to go on with it, and to accomplish it.

For without that grace I can do nothing, but in Thee

I can do all things, when Thy grace doth strengthen me.

O, grace heavenly indeed! without which our most worthy actions are nothing, nor are any gifts of nature to be esteemed.

Neither arts nor riches, beauty nor strength, wit nor eloquence, are any value before Thee, without Thy grace, O Lord.

For gifts of nature are common to good and bad, but the peculiar gift of the elect is grace or love; and they that bear this honorable mark, are accounted worthy of everlasting life.

So eminent is this grace that neither the gift of prophecy, nor the working of miracles, nor any speculation, how high soever is of any esteem without it.

No, not even faith, nor hope, nor any other virtues, are unto Thee acceptable without charity and grace.

O most blessed grace, that makest the poor in spirit rich in virtues and renderest him who is rich in many goods humble in heart!

Come Thou down unto me, come and replenish me early with Thy comfort, lest my soul faint for weariness and dryness of mind.

I beseech Thee, O Lord, that I may find grace in Thy sight; for Thy grace is sufficient for me, though other things that nature desireth be not obtained.

Although I be tempted and vexed with many tribulations, yet I will fear no evil, so long as Thy grace is with me.

This alone and by itself is my strength; this alone giveth advice and help.

This is stronger than all enemies, and wiser than all the wise.

Thy grace is the mistress of truth, the teacher of discipline, the light of the heart, the solace in affliction, the driver away of sorrow, the expeller of fear, the nurse of devotion, the mother of tears.

Without this, what am I but a withered branch, and an unprofitable stock only meet to be cast away!

Let Thy grace therefore, O Lord, always prevent and follow me."

"Like beacon-lights in harbors, which kindling a great blaze by means of a few fagots afford sufficient aid to vessels that wander over the sea, so also a man of bright character in a storm-tossed city, himself content with little, effects great blessings for his fellow-citizens."

"What good did Helvidius Priscus do in resisting Vespasian being but a single person? What good does the purple do on the garment? Why it is splendid in itself, and splendid also in the example which it affords."

"What ought not to be done, do not even think of doing."

"In doing aught which thou hast clearly discerned as right to do, seek never to avoid being seen in the doing of it, even though the multitude should be destined to form some wrong opinion concerning it. For if thou dost not right avoid the deed itself. But if rightly, why fear those who will wrongly rebuke thee."

"Where the glory of God is not made the end of government it is not a legitimate sovereignty, but a usurpation. And he is deceived who expects lasting prosperity in that Kingdom which is not ruled by the sceptre of God."

"No religious services can be transferred to any other than God alone, without committing sacrilege. At first, indeed, superstition ascribed Divine honours either to the sun or to the stars, or to idols. Afterwards followed ambition, which, adorning men with the spoils of God, dared to profane every thing that was sacred. And although there remained a persuasion, that they ought to worship a supreme God, yet it became customary to offer sacrifices promiscuously to genii, and inferior deities, and deceased heroes. So steep is the descent to this vice, to communicate to a vast multitude that which God particularly challenges to Himself alone!"

"We prepare ourselves for sudden deeds by the reiterated choice of good or evil which gradually determines character."

"The growing good of the world is partly dependent on unhistoric acts; and that things are not so ill with you and and me as they might have been, is half owing to the number who lived faithfully a hidden life, and rest in unvisited tombs."

"For the evil will of man makes not a people's good except by stirring the righteous will of man, and beneath all the clouds with which our thought encompasses the Eternal, this is clear—that a people can be blessed only by having counselors and a multitude whose will moves in obedience to the laws of justice and love."

"Every matter hath two handles—by the one it may be

carried, by the other not. If thy brother do thee wrong, take not this thing by the handle, He wrongs me; for that is the handle whereby it may not be carried. But take it rather by the handle, He is my brother, nourished with me; and thou wilt take it by the handle whereby it may be carried."

"Fontenelle says, 'I bow before a great man, but my mind does not bow.' I would add, before an humble plain man, in whom I perceive uprightness of character in a higher degree than I am conscious of in myself, my mind bows whether I choose it or not, and though I bear my head never so high that he may not forget my superior rank. Why is this? Because his example exhibits to me a law that humbles my self-conceit when I compare it with my conduct: a law, the *practicability* of obedience to which I see proved by fact before my eyes. Now, I may even be conscious of a like degree of uprightness, and yet the respect remains. For since in man all good is defective, the law made visible by an example still humbles my pride, my standard being furnished by a man whose imperfections, whatever they may be, are not known to me as my own are, and who therefore appears to me in a more favorable light. *Respect* is a *tribute* which we cannot refuse to merit, whether we will or not; we may indeed outwardly withhold it, but we cannot help feeling it inwardly."

"Not with uncertain, but with assured consciousness do I love Thee, O Lord, Thou hast stricken my heart with Thy word, and I love Thee. And also the heaven, and earth, and all that is therein, behold on every side they say that I should love Thee; nor do they cease to speak unto all, 'so that they are without excuse.' But more profoundly wilt Thou have mercy on whom Thou wilt have mercy, and compassion on whom Thou wilt have compassion, otherwise do both heaven and earth tell forth Thy praises to deaf ears. But what is it that I love in loving Thee? Not corporeal beauty, nor the splendour of tune, nor the radiance of the light, so pleasant to our eyes, nor the sweet melodies of songs of all kinds. nor the fragrant smell of flowers, and ointments, and spices, manna and honey, not limbs pleasant to the embracements of flesh. I love not these things when I love my God; and yet I love a certain kind of light, and sound, and fragrance. and food. and embracement in loving my God, who is light, sound, fragrance, food, and embracement of my inner man—where that light shineth into my soul which no place can contain, where that soundeth which time snatcheth not away, where there is a fragrance which no breeze disperseth, where there is a food which no eating can diminish and where that clingeth which no satiety can sunder. This is what I love, when I love my God. And what is this? I asked the earth; and it answered, 'I am not He;' and whatsoever are therein made the same confession. I asked the sea and the deep and the creeping things that are therein and they replied, 'We are not God. seek higher than we.' I asked the breezy air, and the universal air with its inhabitants answered, 'Anaximenes was deceived. I am not God.' I asked the heavens, the sun, moon, and stars. 'Neither,' say they, 'are we the God whom thou seekest.' And I answered unto all these things which stand about the door of my flesh, 'Ye have told me concerning my God. that ye are not He; tell me something about him.' And with a loud voice they exclaimed, 'He made us.' . . . And I directed my thoughts unto myself and said, 'Who art thou?' And I answered, 'A man.' And lo in me there appeared both body and soul, the one without, the other within. By which of these should I seek my God, whom I had sought through the body from earth to heaven, as far as I was able to send messengers—the beams of mine eyes? But the better part is that which is inner; for to it as both president and judge, did all these corporeal messengers render the answers of heaven and earth and all things therein who said, 'We are not God, but He made us.' These things was my inner man cognizant of by the ministry of the outer. . . . O my soul, thou art my better part, unto thee I speak for thou animatest the mass of my body, but my God is even unto thee the Life of life."

Before the Protestant Reformation the Scriptures were not available to the great body of the people. So even to-day in a real sense the Word of God is not made available through the churches to the people, or at best only a small portion of that Word. How long must it be that the churches will center their study and devotion around the Bible only, and if people learn at all of God's messages through other literature they must do so either contrary to or at least apart from church services and church instruction?

The quotations in this chapter are only a very few of many that could be given. In short to summarize, this chapter has for its purpose to state and to show that the words of James Russell Lowell and of Thomas Carlyle are to be taken to heart literally and not treated as mere poetry or mere fancy.

"Thou hear'st not well the mountain organ-tones
By prophet ears from Hor and Sinai caught,
Thinking the cisterns of those Hebrew brains
Drew dry the springs of the All-knower's thought,
Nor shall thy lips be touched with living fire,
Who blow'st old altar coals with sole desire
To weld anew the spirit's broken chains.

*   *   *   *   *   *

Slowly the Bible of the race is writ,
And not on paper leaves nor leaves of stone;
Each age, each kindred adds a verse to it,
Texts of despair or hope, of joy or moan.
While swings the sea, while mists the mountains shroud,
While thunder's surges burst on cliffs of cloud;
Still at the prophet's feet the nations sit."

"Hast thou well considered all that lies in this immeasurable froth ocean we name *Literature?* Fragments of a genuine Church-Homiletic lie scattered there which time will assort: nay, fractions even of a Liturgy could I point out."

"Men believe in Bibles, and disbelieve in them: but of all Bibles the frightfulest to disbelieve in is this 'Bible of Universal History.' This is the eternal Bible and God's Book 'which every born man,' till once the soul and eye-. sight are extinguished in him, 'can and must, with his own eyes, see the God's-Finger writing.' To discredit this, is an infidelity like no other."

CHAPTER X

The phrase *Kingdom of God* is a Biblical one, found mostly in the Gospels, but by no means confined to them. We find the idea of God's Kingdom in the Old Testament, as well as in the New,—e.g., In Psa. 103:19 we read, "Jehovah hath established his throne in the heaven: And his kingdom ruleth over all." This exalted conception is to be sure a comparatively late development; for modern historical criticism of the Old Testament has shown the religious ideas, there to be found, to have been gradually developed. The Hebrews did not at first consider Yaweh as God of all the earth. So in the song of Moses. we read, "Who is like unto thee, O Jehovah, among the Gods?"*—or again in the message of Jephthah to the children of Ammon, "Wilt not thou possess that which Chemosh thy God giveth thee to possess? So whomsoever Jehovah our God hath dispossessed from before us, them will we possess."** As Prof. W. R. Smith says, speaking of the religion brought in by Moses, "There was a great difference between the religion of Israel and other religions, but that difference cannot be reduced to an abstract formula; it lay in the personal difference, if I may so speak, between Jehovah and the gods of the nations, and all that lay in it only came out bit by bit in the course of a history which was ruled by Jehovah's providence and shaped by Jehovah's love,"†

---

* Exodus 15:11.
** Judges 11:24.
† "The Prophets of Israel," page 52.

Not even did the Hebrews always exclude the worship of other gods in Palestine itself. The great work of Elijah was to clearly and forcibly preach the jealousy of Yaweh —he alone was God of the Hebrews. It was left to later times to extend this idea. Amos seems to have been the one who first plainly and emphatically taught that Yaweh was a universal God of righteousness. "Are ye not as the children of the Ethiopians unto me, O children of Israel? saith Jehovah. Have not I brought up Israel out of the land of Egypt and the Philistines from Caphtor and the Syrians from Kir?" * It would be an interesting study of itself to trace through the Hebrew prophets the development of the idea of God and his rule of the world, but this is beyond the scope of the present chapter.

The Kingdom of God is the central feature of the teaching of Jesus. There is one thing to be noted here however,—the common Jewish conception at this time was apocalyptic. The Jews thought that some great catastrophe would come, then afterwards would be established on the earth the Messianic Kingdom, with Jerusalem as the seat of earthly glory. How far John the Baptist and Jesus shared the apocalyptic view is a question upon which scholars are disagreed. But the thing of importance for us now is the marked superiority of the teaching of Jesus to that of the scribes and even to that of John the Baptist. The burden of Jesus' message was the nearness of the *Kingdom of Heaven,*—just what was meant by this is, as I have said, a matter for further investigation; but the conclusion which Jesus drew from his belief in this nearness was the need of preparation on the part of man for this kingdom. Here it is that Jesus

---

* Amos 9:7.

surpasses even John the Baptist, who preached repentance, and justice between man and man. Dr. O. Holtzmann gives as characteristic of the teaching of Jesus,
"Whether one is a friend of the Messiah, so can hope for
a place in the Kingdom of Heaven, that depends only
upon the measure of readiness to help which he shows
towards others."* The character of the work of Jesus is
seen in his life, and in his teaching that only by loving
trustful submission to God's will and faith in Him, leading
to a life of service and love to one's fellow men, could a
place in the heavenly kingdom be attained.

But even after all the prophets, and the teaching of
Jesus as well, still as Dr. Lyman Abbott well brings
out, when Paul went out to preach to the Gentiles, a large
body of the Christian Church still clung to the idea of
national Jewish election. "In short the Hebrews believed in what seems to us a very narrow doctrine of
election; they believed that religion was only for the Jews,
and God was the God of the Jews only."**

Considerably later "in the Catholic church composed
as it was in unequal parts of Jews and Gentiles, the doctrine soon became dominant that God is the God if all the
baptized."† That this is so Dante well illustrates. "So
he set forth and so he made me enter within the first
circle that girds the abyss. Here, so far as could be
heard, there was no plaint but that of sighs which made
the eternal air tremble: this came of the woe without
torments felt by the crowds, which were many and great,
of infants and of women and of men. The good Master

---

* Holtzmann's "Leben Jesu," page 135.
** Lyman Abbott, "The Rights of Man," page 34.
† Lyman Abbott, "The Rights of Man," page 34.

(meaning Virgil) to me, 'Thou dost not ask what spirits are these thou seest. Now I would have thee know, before thou goest farther, that they sinned not; if they have merits it sufficeth not, because they had not baptism, which is part of the faith that thou believest; and if they were before Christianity, they did not duly worship God. . . . Through such defects, and not through other guilt, are we lost and only so far harmed that without hope we live in desire."*

Calvinistic election had the possibility at least of developing into a broader principle. Again in the rise of Methodism, we have a still wider election. "It is, in a word, that God chooses all who choose Him. God is regarded as the Father not merely of a race, a baptized, an elect, but of all who, accepting his gift of life, become conscious sharers of that life with Him."** This choice on the part of man was however supposed to be a violent break with one's past life. Man grew up away from God. Especially was salvation to be had only through Jesus Christ. He was believed to be the only way to God. Only by accepting his sacrifice, was salvation to be had. A still wider conception than this of early Methodism is now before us,—namely that God is the Father of all, that He not only accepts all who choose Him, but He desires all men everywhere to choose Him and that He is Father of the wayward and erring and sinful, even as of the righteous. And the way of salvation is through God Himself, who is not far from any one of us,

---

* Lyman Abbott, "The Rights of Man," pages 35-36, quoted there from Dante's Inferno, Canto 5. C. E. Norton's translation.
** Lyman Abbott, "The Rights of Man," page 38.

rather than through any belief in or even knowledge of Jesus.

Now that we have traced the widening conception of God's Kingdom, before taking up more in detail the scope of this kingdom, it will be instructive perhaps to note a common weakness of those pictures of ideal states which men have fashioned for themselves. Take for example such ideal representation as *Plato's Republic, More's Utopia,* or, coming down to a later time, *Bellamy's Looking Backward.* These differ among themselves, but all have certain common features, both good and bad. All these are, in the first place, books of the times in which they were written. They are criticisms as well upon existing states, as ideals for the future. What seems to be a common weakness in them all is that authority is too apt to be made external. The visible political machinery is too much emphasized. In *Plato's Republic,* the family life is too lightly esteemed; *More's Utopia* and *Bellamy's Looking Backward* fall into the fatal error of leveling downward. By taking away the loftiest ideals, or subordinating them, they take away the most important springs of action. This is why we believe that any such attempt to picture a perfect society is sure to fail. Rather must we say that the heart of man can not imagine the future which is possible to the race.

These books which we have mentioned can however teach us a useful lesson, if we will but learn it,—namely that the *Kingdom of God* is not merely a far away ideal, nor merely a matter of what we commonly and perhaps narrowly call religion. *The Kingdom of God* must embrace and include physical, political and social well-being.

The very fact that men are seeking after these things makes it clear that these desires must be either suppressed or in some way satisfied, before there can be an ideal condition. The view of Tolstoi leads to suppression of ambition by his doctrine of extreme simplicity and altruism. Pessimism, such as that of Schopenhauer,—desire is the cause of misery,—also leads to the same advice—suppress all desires. There is the extreme opposite view, well represented by the writings of Nietzsche—the doctrine of the survival of the strong, and suppression of the weak. There is struggle for existence in the strict sense. A man's life is made to consist of that which he hath.

Neither of these positions satisfies either the human intellect or the human heart. This leads us to a further study of the *Kingdom of God,* having in view not only man's religious life, but his whole civilization. For justification of this point of view, we have only to turn to philosophy. The time was when there were lords many and gods many, the age of polytheism. Then followed the age of dualism—whether absolute or partial. This was probably a common conception among many of the Jews about the time of Jesus. God was supreme, but the world was given over to Satan for the time being. Messiah was to come, *bind the strong men and spoil his goods.* Then would be set up the *Kingdom of God.* A similar dualistic idea is to be found in Plato, in a different form, to be sure, in his conception of flesh and matter as evil. With monistic theism, however, spirit is the fundamental reality,—mind and matter are both grounded in the one being whom we call God. All things are then eternally parts of the *Kingdom of God.* Neither material progress, art, music, literature, or culture are born of evil, though all may, of course, be wrongly used. What we do say is they are not inherently bad, but good. Let us then consider six great elements of civilization,—government, industry, science, culture, ethics and religion.

Government: First of all, let us turn to government. If one were to ask the reason why the doctrine of evolution was and is still so distasteful to many, the answer would doubtless be because it seems to give all our cherished possessions such a low and degraded origin. This is true not only in the physiological realm but also in the governmental as well. In "Physics and Politics" or, as he also calls it, "thoughts on the application of the principles of natural selection and inheritance to political society," Bagehot traces the gradual development of government and our political ideas. He there tries to show and succeeds fairly well in showing that first of all we have the patriarchal rule with kinship as the bond of union, that the stronger this bond was the more likely the family was to survive. This required absolute obedience and subordination. In the words of Bagehot, "law, rigid, definite, concise law is the primary want of early mankind; that which they need above everything else, that which is requisite before they can gain anything else."* There is now "natural selection" pure and simple,— one clan more firmly bound together than others survives, others perish. Obedience is the main thing; he who innovates or questions is criminal, traitor, heretic.— to death with him! So what is called a "cake of custom" is formed. Today we see many tribes who have not advanced beyond this stage. Isolation is necessary. "Who-

---

* "Physics and Politics," page 19.

ever speaks two languages is a rascal" well shows the early feeling. Commerce is the great enemy of this established order, and is held in low repute, sometimes being forbidden.

Three laws or "approximate laws" from Bagehot give us an interesting view—

"First—in every particular state of the world those nations which are strongest tend to prevail over the others; and in certain marked peculiarities the strongest tend to be the best.

Secondly—Within every particular nation the type or types of character then and there most attractive tend to prevail, and the most attractive, though with exceptions, is what we call the best character.

Thirdly—Neither of these competitions is in most historic conditions intensified by extrinsic force, but in some conditions such as those now prevailing in the most influential part of the world both are so intensified"*

It is no wonder that so many are loathe to accept such as the origin of government. What in a word is this theory? It is that government was developed by war and conquest, that by the best we mean strongest. "Might makes right." Such a view certainly gives rise to such definitions of government as that of Tolstoi. "Government," says he, "is organized violence."** If this view is once adopted, it is impossible to predict the consequences. "Government is organized violence." Then what difference between government and the anarchist save that one has more power than the other?

Men seeing to what this view leads have tried to give

* "Physics and Politics," page 43.
** "Slavery of our Times," page 129.

other explanations of government, its nature and origin. Among these we have the social compact theory as an attempt to reconcile government and justice. We simply note the following objections here in passing.

(1) All historic evidence is against it. This objection is a very great one; for as Woodrow Wilson points out in "The State" the question of the origin of government is a question of fact demanding historical research rather than philosophical speculation.*

(2) Even though it were true that there was originally a compact, the descendants of these first men ought not, at least according to our ideas of justice, to be bound by the original agreement.

(3) The list of names of those who have held this theory or advocated it shows how it can be used to justify nearly any form of government. Hobbes could use it as his justification for absolutism, as well as Rousseau for his *return to nature and a state of freedom.*

(4) By this theory justice is made dependent upon its acceptability. Government is not accepted because just, but is just because accepted.—This is what the social compact theory leads to.

What then shall we say of the origin of government? It cannot be denied surely that it has often developed through war and oppression, bloodshed, tyranny and craft. Aristotle says "Man is a political animal." Aristotle** gives three prinicipal types of government,—monarchy, rule of one; aristocracy rule of the best; democracy, rule of the people, the many.

---

* For the origin of government and objections to compact theory, see "The State," by Woodrow Wilson, chapter 1.
** Wilson, "The State," page 599.

Monarchy theoretically, rests on the divine descent, or at least the divine right of one man to rule in the place of God, as his representative on earth. Obligarchy is but an extension of the idea of monarchy,—one family or a few families represent the law. Aristocracy says fitness to govern, knowledge, experience, point us out as the interpreters of the divine law. But what is democracy? Woodrow Wilson says, "Vox legis, vox populi." *

Industry and Society: Here it seems best to present a summary of the view of Mallock as set forth in "Aristocracy and Evolution." After criticism of the modern sociological method, the author goes on to state the position of those whom he criticizes, Mr. Kidd and Mr. Spencer. The position of the latter he sums up as follows,—"The causes, says Mr. Spencer, of all social phenomena are physical environment and men's natural character. The first physical cause of progress was an exceptionally fertile soil and an exceptionally bracing climate. All the conquering races came from fertile and bracing regions. There were other regions more fertile, but these were enervating; and hence the inhabitants of the former enslaved the weaker inhabitants of the latter. Again, division of labour, on which industrial progress depends, was caused by difference in the products of different localities, which led to the localization of industries. The localization of industries in its turn led to road making; and roads made possible the centralization of authority and interchange of ideas. Next, as to men's natural character, which is the other cause of progress, their primitive character did not fit them to progress. till it was

---

* Wilson, "The State," page 619.

gradually improved by the evolution of marriage and the family especially of monogamy. Monogamy represents the survival of the fittest kind of sexual union. It developed the affections and the practice of efficient co-operation. The family being established, the nation gradually rose from it. One family increased, and gave rise tó many families, which were obliged, in order to get food to separate into different groups; and the recompounding of these groups, for purposes of defence or aggression, formed the nation; all government being in its origin military. But as the arts of life progress, industry emancipates itself from governmental control, and becomes its own master, and also forms the basis of political democracy."*

Mr. Mallock objects to the carrying on of this same method to the present age. True, says he, evolution such as here described probably did once take place, but now we see a different state of things.—not only is there an "unintended progress", evolution pure and simple; but "great men" produce "intended results." These latter are continually becoming more and more important. Progress is no longer the result of a struggle for mere existence or life, but for "domination". It is the few who struggle for this "domination" and who promote progress primarily. But what motives lead a man to exert great efforts, to produce industrial progress? This leads us to note the power of such a man, for as Mallock says, "A large number of the great works of antiquity were due to labour successfully stimulated by the whip. But it is only a man's commonest faculties that can be called intó action thus; and they can be called into action thus only

* "Aristocracy and Evolution" by Mallock, see page IX.

for this reason that those who coerce him know that these faculties are possessed by him, and they also know the task which they wish him to accomplish. But in the case of the great man both these conditions are wanting. . . . Any farmer by looking at Burns could have told that he had the makings of a ploughman in him, and have forced him, under certain circumstances, to do so much ploughing daily; but no one could have told that he was a poet if he had not of his own free will revealed the fact to the public; and even then when the public were aware of it, no one could have forced him to compose "The Cotter's Saturday Night." A press gang could have turned Columbus into a common sailor, but not all the sovereigns of Europe could have forced him to discover a new hemisphere."* So it is with the entrepreneur; in a certain very real sense he has power to do or not to do. The public is dependent upon him. If then he is struggling selfishly only for the gratification of his own ambition, what then?

Science: This is an age of science, hence any account of civilization must take this into consideration. Perhaps we cannot do better than look briefly at Tyndall's famous *Belfast Address on the Advancement of Science.* The scientific impulse he says is inherent in man from the first, but in primitive times all explanations of phenomena were anthropomorthic; only gradually did man become able to eliminate the personal equation and seek by observation and experiment to know things as they are in themselves. Tyndall traces the beginnings of science among the Greeks to Democritus, Empedocles, and Epicurus. Lucretius the Roman carried on the work. Dur-

---

* "Aristocracy and Evolution." pages 277-278.

ing the Middle Ages in Europe the spirit of enquiry was suppressed. Authority whether of the Bible as interpreted by the Church or of Aristotle was blindly followed. During this period, what science there was is to be found among the Arabs. A revival came in Europe, however, under Copernicus, Bruno, Galileo, Bacon, Kepler, Newton, Descartes, Hobbes, Gassendi and others.

During the last century this movement has been coming to its full life, so that at present it is difficult on the one hand to realize how great an advance has been made, and on the other the full significance of recent discoveries with their future influence on civilization. Darwin, Wallace and Huxley represent the great doctrine of evolution. The same principles carried over into psychology led Mr. Spencer to define life as a "continuous adjustment of internal relations to external relations." To what then do all these things lead? Tyndall himself says, "The questions here raised are inevitable. They are approaching us with accelerated speed, and it is not a matter of indifference whether they are introduced with reverence or irreverence. Abandoning all disguise, the confession that I feel bound to make before you is that I prolong the vision backward across the boundary of the experimental evidence, and discover in that matter, which we in our ignorance, and notwithstanding our professed reverence for its Creator, have hitherto covered with opprobrium, the promise and the potency of every form and quality of life."*

The conception would be very inadequate which we should get of Tyndall if we stopped here. A little later we will go back to him and get his larger view. Our

---

* Tyndall, "Advancement of Science," page 77.

reason for stopping here now is that so many students of science do stop here.

Ethics: We have thus far taken up government, sociology, and science from a one-sided standpoint. It would be unfair to suppose however that, even had we fully covered these topics, we would have completed the whole range of our subject. Ethics, aesthetics, and religion yet remain to be considered. While the views of political and economic life we have thus far presented seem to lead to hedonistic ethics, the same cannot be said in equal degree of science even on the materialistic basis. For here conformity to law is above all emphasized, and this law is the law of truth,—for no matter what is regarded as the source of truth, without this belief in truth and the possibility of knowing the truth, there can be no science. This is so self-evident as scarcely to need argument. Science which so many orthodox Christian writers seem to fear, or hate, or despise, as the case may be, is one of the strongest and most potent grounds for belief in God. If we have science, belief in God follows of necessity. Unless we believe in God, even in a metaphysical sense, as the source and ground of truth how can we believe in the possibility of science? Kant finds moral law within man himself. There is a noumenal within man and commanding him. In this way we have a God of stern justice and unbending law. As Schurman puts it science gives us a *God* of *Sinai.*

Aesthetics: But ethics is not all. Man has not only the feeling of law and restraint, but an aesthetical nature also. Victor Hugo well brings out this truth in his book entitled "William Shakespeare." Hugo makes a clear distinction between Science and Art which is I believe at least

partially true. He says, "Among human things, and inasmuch as it is a human thing, Art is a strange exception. . . . Now progress is the motive of science;
the ideal is the generator of Art. . . . Art progresses
after its own fashion, it shifts its ground, like Science;
but its successive creations containing the unchangeable,
abide; while the admirable guesses of Science, which are
and can be nothing but combinations of the contingent,
obliterate each other."* "Science seeks perpetual motion.
She has found it; it is Science herself."** "Science is
the asymptote of truth; it approaches unceasingly, and
never touches."†

Religion: True art then leads us to religion by its
emphasis upon and partaking of the ideal factor. Religion is the crown and completion of all sides of civilization. We have taken up government, society, and science
leaving out religion. Let us now go back and take a
broader and a truer view.

We saw in discussion of government that democracy
says, "Vox Legis; vox populi."‡ The democracy, where
there is liberty, equality, and fraternity must extend this
and say, *vox legis, vox populi, vox dei.* All men are
equal before the law because all men *live and move* and
have their being in one God. Before Him all are equal,
—equal in what? Not in attainment, or wealth, or health,
or thought, or life—no, equal only in the sense of being
each and every one an expression of the divine life. Each
one is responsible for himself, each one is a free moral

---

* "William Shakespeare" by Victor Hugo, pages 101-102.
** "William Shakespeare" by Victor Hugo, page 105.
† "William Shakespeare" by Victor Hugo, page 114.
‡ Wilson "The State," page 619.

agent, each one has certain rights of life and of liberty. To sum up the whole matter, true democracy says man is a rational being and "if", to quote from Tolstoi, "men are rational beings, their relations should be based on reason and not on the violence of those who happen to have seized power."*

Many there are who believe that the highest and best form of government yet devised is a representative republic. Not all men can become specialists in government, any more than in law or in medicine. But he who believes in God as the Supreme Ruler in truth and in righteousness, "will follow only the leader who has himself allegiance to the truth and who has sought and found it."** "Even if they cannot become specialists, they are like those medical patients who know the difference between a quack and an authority, and put themselves under the guidance of those who are competent to lead. We cannot make all men specialists in philosophy, but I see no reason why all men should not have philosophical standards of work and insist that the authors and reformers and political leaders who receive their confidence or their support shall be earnest seekers after truth, shall weigh evidence instead of dogmatize, shall critically analyze deep problems and get at fundamental principles instead of being side-tracked on unimportant issues."†

So too in sociology, we can get a loftier view than before,—for to go back to Mr. Mallock, he says, "In order to see how the great man promotes progress, we must consider that whilst the fittest survivor only promotes it

---

* "Slavery of Our Times," by Tolstoi, page 142.
** "Letters, Lectures and Addresses" by Garman, page 88.
† "Letters, Lectures and Addresses" by Garman, page 92.

by living, whilst thus die, the great man promotes progress by helping others to live. He promotes progress not
by what he does himself, but by what he helps other to
do."* He criticises the current sociology. It has, he says,
tried to deal with two classes of questions, speculative and
practical. With the former it has been successful; in the
case of the latter it has failed. And why has it failed?
Because it has not taken due account of the difference between Darwinian and moral evolution,—in a word it has
merged the individual into the "aggregate." Prof. Garman made the following contrast between Darwinian and
moral evolution.** Under the former there is struggle
for existence, the weak perish, there is no hope for the
individual, progress is extremely slow; under the latter
there is struggle not for existence but for righteousness, if
any perish it is the strong who perish for the weak, there
is hope for the individual, progress may be rapid under
certain conditions.

So in the realm of science if we return to Tyndall's
Belfast Address we read these words, spoken it would
seem to give Mr. Spencer's position, but with Tyndall's
approval. "Our states of consciousness are mere symbols
of an outside entity, which produces them and determines
the order of their succession, but the real nature of which
we can never know. In fact, the whole process of evolution is the manifestation of a Power absolutely inscrutable
to the intellect of man. As little in our day as in the days
of Job can man, by searching, find this Power out."† This
is an advance over materialism. But Tyndall goes fur-

---

* "Aristocracy and Evolution," page XV.
** In lectures at Amherst College.
† "Advancement of Science." pages 78-79.

ther. "Then there are such things woven into the texture of man as the feeling of awe, reverence, wonder—and not alone the sexual love just referred to (this reference I have not quoted but Tyndall has just been speaking of the priority of this impulse), but the love of the beautiful, physical and moral, in nature, poetry, and art. There is also that deep-set feeling which since the earliest dawn of history, and probably for ages prior to all history incorporated itself in the religions of the world."*

What in a word then is the position of science? It is, I think, that systems of cosmogony are a peculiar realm for itself—free investigation must here be allowed. In the realm of religion also truth is an essential element; but even the scientist recognizes that the truth is only a part, though a necessary part of religion. As Tyndall says, "The world embraces not only a Newton, but a Shakespeare; not only a Boyle, but a Raphael; not only a Kant but a Beethoven; not only a Darwin but a Carlyle. Not in each of these, but in all, is human nature whole. They are not opposed, but supplementary; not mutually exclusive, but reconcilable."†

So in ethics, the law of duty in the heart of man from the religious standpoint is God speaking to man. In art, too, we have the religious element not only in the ideal factor, but ethics joins with aesthetics and gives the true motive for the beautiful. Neither science nor art is for its own sake, but for the sake of man. As Hugo says, "It is important, at the present time, to bear in mind that the human soul has still greater need of the ideal

---

* "Advancement of Science," pages 81-82.
† "Advancement of Science," page 87.

than of the real. It is by the real that we exist; it is by the ideal that we live."*

Religion we have not yet taken up separately. Here we must distinguish between the spread of some form of religion throughout the world and religion from the standpoint of the individual. We are not here particularly interested in discussing the spread of any one religion or its rites and ceremonies. In considering the *Kingdom of God* on earth we are not primarily, if at all, interested in these. What we have thus far been endeavoring to show is that we look forward to government founded on reason not on violence, society saved and regenerated by service, science developing for man, until he shall be *the head* and *not the hand,* and until sickness and disease shall be no more. In this connection, if there were time, it would be interesting to trace the wonderful progress of surgery and medicine; in the latter such work as that of Koch and of Pasteur, as well as of more recent specialists, certainly promises remarkable things, and these are but beginnings.

Religion: From the realm of ethics and art, we are led to religion because only in God do we find the true source of all. This is why we assign to religion last place; —because it crowns all and unites all. Only by faith and trust and love can all these other things be controlled and guided in such a way as not to be curses rather than blessings. In the last analysis man is dependent directly on God. To Him he lives—to Him he is responsible. Here and here alone do we find the unity possible not only for science, ethics and art, but also for all human friendships

---

* "William Shakespeare," page 295.

and relationships. Let us then ask what in a word is religion. It is a personal communion between God and man. God reveals Himself to man and so redeems man by a vision of Himself—vision of Himself as governor of the world in reason, as giver of all material prosperity, as source of truth, as the one who implants within man his moral nature, and gives to the heart of man, the longing for the ideal, and supremely as redeemer of man revealing Himself to man through the lives of men and women, when they show forth the highest of all qualities, faith, hope and love, and so drawing man to Himself by the *at-one-ment of mercy.* Man then lives in faith toward God, and in the spirit of humble trust.

To emphasize once more the abiding and enduring elements of religion which is a matter between God and man directly they are:

(1)   Faith in God—trustful submission to His will as to the will of a loving Father who knows what is best for His children, but with full realization that submission to His will requires active use of all the powers He gives us.

(2)   Hope—founded on reason, hope for the future, time and eternity, because of faith.

(3)   Love—to God and love to man, this love being shown in a life of service. As Hugo says, "Help from the strong for the weak, help from the great for the small, help from the free for the slaves, help from the thinkers for the ignorant, help from the solitary for the multitudes."*

Faith, hope, and love,—these constitute true religion, and these alone bring the *Kingdom of God* to pass on

---

* "William Shakespeare," page 318.

earth by first bringing it into the hearts and lives of men. *The Kingdom of God comes without observation,*—it comes first of all within man. Faith toward God, hope in His constant help and care, love toward God and man, —these were at the foundation of the religion of Jesus, who taught both by precept and by life submission to God's will, who dared to hope all things and taught his disciples *to receive the Kingdom of God* in the spirit of little children, and who gave as the rule of service and law of love, "Love your enemies, and pray for them that persecute you; that you may be sons of your Father who is in heaven."* "Ye therefore shall be perfect, as your heavenly Father is perfect."†

At the present time it seems especially necessary to emphasize the unity and the universality of religion. Such terms as Christian religion, Buddhist religion are in a sense contradictory terms. The minute we begin to qualify and restrict religion or speak as if men, or nations or races of men were shut out from God's love and care, we leave true religion. Justice, mercy and love are not to be qualified by national or racial adjectives. The very essence of religion is "the life of God in the soul of man." It seems sacrilege to us all to speak seriously as though there were a Christian religion or life of God, or an American religion or life of God, distinct and sharply differentiated from religion itself.

In a sense, all of the elements of our civilization, our government, industrial relations, science, ethics, aesthetics and religion are human and imperfect. None of them

---

* Matthew 5:44-45.
† Matthew 5:48.

have been presented to us in complete, perfect and authoritative form.   We do affirm however in all positiveness that justice, sovereignty, truth, and art, are all divine in origin, and in their development.   Unless they all as well as our own lives are grounded in God, they do not exist at all. But if we do live and move and have our being in God, then it becomes of supreme importance to view all things in God.   Then to live is to be religious.

"Outward Religion originates by Society, Society becomes possible by Religion.   Nay, perhaps, every conceivable Society, past and present, may well be figured as properly and wholly a Church, in one or other of these three predicaments: an audibly preaching and prophesying Church, which is the best: second, a Church that struggles to preach and prophesy, but cannot as yet, till its Pentecost come; and third and worst, a church gone dumb with old age, or which only mumbles delirium prior to dissolution.   Whoso fancies that by Church is here meant Chapter-houses and Cathedrals, or by preaching and prophesying mere speech and chanting, let him read on, light of heart."   Carlyle.

"O grace abundant, by which I presumed
To fix my sight upon the Light Eternal,
    *   *   *   *   *   *
I saw that in its depth far down is lying
Bound with love together in one volume,
What through the universe is scattered;
Substance, and accident, and their operations,
All interfused together in such wise
That what I speak of is one simple light.
    *   *   *   *   *   *

In presence of that light one such becomes,
That to withdraw therefrom for other prospect
It is impossible he e'er consent;
Because the good, which object is of will,
Is gathered all in this, and out of it
That is defective which is perfect there."

—DANTE.

CHAPTER XI

In many respects the writer considers the present chapter the most important in this little book, and the most difficult to compile or to write. It is easy to be critical or to catalogue negative knowledge. It is also easy, after once one has attained or arrived at a positive position, to outline that position. It is far more difficult to state clearly and concisely the fundamental reasons for that position, in such a way that another can for himself approach the entire subject understandingly or work out his own belief. Yet difficult as the task before us is, it is not to be shunned, indeed the main purpose of this book culminates in this one chapter.

The writer has all along emphasized the destructive results of historical criticism and has criticized the negative theology of the time. The person without positive belief is to be pitied rather than criticized. The writer knows in his heart that his entire life has been blessed and made worth while to himself at least by that very presentation of philosophical problems that made it forever afterward impossible for him to accept either orthodoxy or modern liberal but negative theology. He shudders to think of what would have been his intellectual and spiritual outlook upon life had Professor Garman never entered into his life. He feels that if any one has in his heart, even as he himself had, a growing doubt and

152

agnosticism, though unexpressed and almost unaware to himself, it is worth any effort to try to set forth the philosophic basis of theology in such a way that that person may receive a vision of God and of truth that will evermore bless his life. If a single indivdual can thus be helped, this book will have served its purpose, no matter how much criticism or indifference it may elsewhere encounter.

No work in all this world, no position nor station in life, no wealth nor any preferment, can, in the opinion of the writer, speaking for himself, even be compared with the duty and the joy of setting forth the philosophic basis of theology. It is the writer's chief regret, and he feels like apologizing for the fact, that he has done so little along this line. While he seems to have been prevented by conditions and circumstances, he is not free from the thought that possibly he could have done more. The philosophic basis for theology as it was presented to him and as it has been pondered and made his own seems to him of such priceless value as to be above words to describe.

In presenting the philosophic basis for theology the writer cannot avoid mention again of Professor Garman. What will here be presented the writer feels was received practically all of it from Professor Garman, but he has made it his own. So it is not presented as the thought or the system of another. I would long hesitate before such an attempt lest I should fail to do justice to that philosophy or to the great teacher. I do however feel not only free but in duty bound to present in this chapter the substance of the great thoughts that first aroused in me deep interest, nay, more than interest, even a very life and death grapple with theology, and which also sustained me as later studies

in the theological seminary took away one inherited belief
after another. This philosophic theology then proved to
be a belief by which I could live and has ever since been
as a well of water of which he who drinks never more
does thirst.

As far as the writer is aware he accepts the philosophical conclusions of Professor Garman practically in their
entirety, not on his authority, but because after the most
rigorous study they seem correct, nay more than correct,
they seem as the very fundamentals of life. The writer
is not conscious of differing therefrom in any important
particular. As for theology as distinguished from philosophy, it is proper to state that its questions were not
directly discussed by Professor Garman in his classes, nor
did the writer have opportunity, during or after his divinity school course, to discuss these problems as he would
like to have done had Professor Garman's life not been so
suddenly cut off in his prime. In the Memorial Volume
already referred to, page 467, in an address to the Amherst class of 1903, Professor Garman distinctly says that
he accepts the doctrine of Christ's divinity and incarnation. From this statement, which however is not believed
to be at all vital to the theistic philosophy of Professor
Garman, the present writer does entirely dissent, unless
he be allowed to use the words divinity and incarnation
in such a way that they can be applied to all great and
good men as well as and in the same sense as to Jesus.

Quite likely I cannot do justice to Professor Garman's
philosophy. Let it then at the outset be clearly understood that this is not an attempt to present it, even although this chapter is largely comprised of quotations
from Professor Garman. The writer only claims to pre-

sent those things which he himself believes in, and which rightly or wrongly he holds to. He freely admits that his own originality lies in only his sincerity, in that he believes these things for himself, rather than that he discovered them or has himself any merit of novelty. He may have misunderstood or misinterpreted Professor Garman, and even if he does understand his philosophy in part, he has not sufficient power of expression adequately to set it forth. Let no one then ascribe to Professor Garman any errors of the writer. If there is anything of good let it be received. And after all, every great teacher, notably Professor Garman, has felt and believed that his permanent influence would be in the attitude of mind and heart that he might arouse in his students rather than in their exact conclusions. It is the spirit rather than the letter that is most worth while.

In attempting a statement of the philosophic basis of theology at this time, only a summary is given. The subject is worthy of more extended treatment than is possible in this *Introduction to Theology*. We will try however to make clear the main outlines which seem so important to the writer.

The central, the fundamental question, is whether we can believe in God, and what it is to so believe. A study of psychology and the mental processes, as well as of biology and the theory of evolution, presents to us all as the central questions and main problems,—Is all thought a function of the brain? Is materialism the correct belief or is there ground for belief in idealism? Study of the brain, and of habit for example, seems to indicate that our thinking is based upon 'experience, and that being based thereon our thinking follows the course of least resistance. Is imitation and the following of brain paths all that there is to our mental life?

Is the every-day world of sense perception the all-in-all of life, or are there grounds for belief in spiritual reality?

"The determining note in Professor Garman's teaching of philosophy was his conception of philosophy. It was not for him primarily a subject to be studied for its own sake. One might say it was not studied as a subject at all. He believed that every man who thinks at all must sooner or later face the alternatives which are represented in general by a spiritual or a materialistic view of the world and of human action. He conceived it his task to aid young men in facing the problem squarely, and with a method for its solution." *

Questions squarely presented were, "Are the laws of thought the laws of things?" and "Are we to be agnostics or theists?"**

These questions are examined in the light of what mankind claims to have, namely,—

(a) Vicarious knowledge, or science, where it is claimed that by study of a part or of the individual specimen we can arrive at universal laws. On what basis do we thus attribute to qualities or laws universality? Do we really have science or must we remain agnostic here?

(b) Vicarious volition, sovereignty, or government.

---

* All quotations in this chapter, unless otherwise stated are from "Letters, Lectures and Addresses of Charles Edward Garman; A Memorial Volume." (Houghton Mifflin Co.) For this quotation see page 31.
** Page 44.

Man claims to legislate for others. On what ground or what basis can an individual or a group of individuals or the state interfere with or determine the action of others? Is it simply a case of might or force, or is there any reasonable ground for the exercise of sovereignty either human or divine?

(c) Vicarious judgment, or justice. This raises the whole question of whether there is justice, and, if so, its basis, and what ground, or justification there is, if any, for punishment of the evil doer.

"Two alternatives confront us; either all mental processes depend wholly upon mechanical laws, or there is thought and action not so determined. Mechanical forces follow lines of least resistance; but if there is any such thing as science at all, thinking must be determined by the test, What is true? This implies conclusions based, not on habit or association or brain paths, but on evidence. In ethical terms the two alternatives are: (a) Darwinian evolution is the whole explanation of man and society. Therefore life is only a struggle for existence with survival of the "fittest." The only motive is self-preference; the only virtue is success; the only vice is failure. (b) Man has a dual nature which on the one hand follows habit and laws of least resistance, but on the other, as a spiritual nature with power to weigh evidence, is governed by entirely different laws making service, not self-preference, the standard of action, and justice, not success, the criterion of virtue." *

"Either all our knowledge comes from experience—more than that, all our ideas either true or false, i. e.,

* Page 50.

our wildest superstitions as truly as science itself, come from experience—or the mind is able to obtain knowledge and ideas outside of and beyond experience."*

"If all our knowledge comes from experience, it seems fair to inquire what are its limits .   .   Is not strict agnosticism. concerning every thing beyond these limits not merely our duty, but also our safety?

"How can the limits of knowledge be determined? Since the days of Kant this question has been answered by an illustration. A child who sees a dove flying in a storm and buffeted by the wind hastily concludes that if only it could get above the atmosphere it would be unhindered, and might easily leave this earth and soar to heaven. But when the child learns how the dove flies at all, when he understands that only through the resistance of the air is the bird borne up and able to move on the wing, then he discovers the limits of its highest flight. Never again can he think of its getting beyond the atmosphere of earth. So when we accurately determine the processes of attaining knowledge we shall realize that all subjects that cannot be brought within these processes are forever beyond our ken. Here, then. is our problem: 'What are the true and only processes by which knowledge is gained?' "**

Professor Garman answers this question by study of a particular case, "viz., just what one must do in order to communicate with his friends, i. e., know the very thoughts. motives and purposes of his most intimate companion at a given time."†

In this there are three stages or processes.

---

* Page 208.
** Pages 209-210.
† Page 210.

(a)   We have what the senses give us.

(b)   "We must use these pictures as data and from them infer their cause. This process is similar to the telegraph clerk's work. She receives from her instrument merely clicks. Upon these she fits the code of the office and then spells out a message. But suppose her code is not the one used by the sender of the message?"*

"The code we use is one expressing the laws of thought, the one stating how the mind itself would have worked if it had created or imagined these sense pictures. No other code is possible for us."**

"If the laws of thought are not known to be the laws of things, how can we ever know things? And can the laws of thought be known to be the laws of things—mark the word, I do not say the laws of thought be the laws of things, but *be known* to be the laws of things—unless we first know that both thought and things are products of the same larger self, whom we call God? Here is my problem. Must we not take this view of our limitations or be absolutely agnostic concerning everything that transcends the smaller self?"†

(c)   "The third step in the process of communicating with our friends comes after we persuade ourselves that we have gained accurate knowledge of the external physical world through the senses. From the physical contact of our friends, i. e., words uttered, expressions of countenance, gestures (what

---

* Page 211.
** Page 215.
† Page 222.

Hume would call superficial properties), we must infer the secret hidden character and motives, distinguish between jest and earnest, knowledge and ignorance, frankness and reserve. This is a scientific problem. Beginning in childhood, and making at first the most embarrassing mistakes, we carefully repeat the inductive process till we get hypotheses that stand criticism, and in time gain confidence that our work is correct. This is our study of human nature. What is its basis? Simply this, if we had done these deeds, uttered these words, hesitated, become excited, then gone off abruptly, we should have had definite embarrassment and no little anger, therefore, our friend felt the same. Here is vicarious knowledge of his mind following on vicarious knowlege of his external physical deeds. If all beings are separate and independent entities, we ought to have an agnosticism raised (lowered, possibly, would be more accurate) to the second power concerning the mental life of friends. But this is just the one thing we are most confident of. That and only that makes life worth living. Did an agnostic ever live who really doubted this knowledge? Why do agnostics publish books to prove their doctrine? Why do they answer up so sharply when criticized? How know that others meant by those words what they interpret them to mean? No, men are not agnostic on this subject. Not that we know all about others, but that we do know something of their thought and of the intent of their hearts. The phrases mother, father, mean this or they are mere mockeries. To be really agnostic on this question would be out and out insanity. So long as a spark of life glows in us we shall hold to our faith in our ability to read the thoughts of other members of the human race when we have adequate data. Some are quicker and keener than we in this work, but even a woman's intuitions are no miraculous power. The process so far as it may be carried is always and everywhere inductive. or when this has been completed and we simply apply its results, deductive. There is only one possible ground on which it can rest, viz., that we know human nature as truly as physical nature to be uniform with our own conscious processes. Given this cognition and the path is so plain that the wayfaring man, even though a pluralist, need not err therein; but without this cognition the greatest genius is helpless. Indeed, the clearer his mental vision the quicker will he realize his isolation from every one else."*

"But here is the old question. How is the pluralist going to know that other human beings are uniform with himself? Must he not logically believe in monism and refuse to consider the world as made up of separate independent entities? Is there any other possible ground for the conviction that our true thought processes, and therefore our laws of thought. are universal?"**

To sum up the subject thus far, unless things and ourselves are both grounded and have their being in God, we have no science, to say nothing of sovereignty and justice, nay we are each one of us in "solitary confinement for eternity," we must ever be agnostic about all other

---

* Pages 222-223.   ** Page 224.

persons and things. The only basis upon which we can live at all a sane mental life is on the monistic theistic basis.

"If a man is honestly searching for the truth, the whole truth, and nothing but the truth, can he logically be confident about the objective existence and purposes of his friends but agnostic concerning God, the true self on whom all are dependent? Logically, are we not more sure of the existence of this Being and of some, not all, of the processes and laws that govern His actions, than we are of the existence of a physical world and of our ability to communicate with our companions. Until we are sure of this Being and of the dependence of all things upon Him, can we be sure that our inferences really take us beyond the subjective? Some hesitate to rest on these conclusions. There is no flaw in the logic, but they are afraid of anthropomorphism. If God were an absentee deity, living off somewhere in the distance from us. we should be anthropomorphic in ascribing to Him laws that govern us. We should not have a vestige of evidence to base such predicates upon. But if we are His workmanship more truly than the swinging of the pendulum is the work of gravity, the case is different. Our inner life is a laboratory where His processes are revealed. Uniformity under the same conditions is tautology. We are not predicating human attributes of God, but divine attributes of man, simply affirming that man partakes of the divine nature, is made in the image of God. This is not anthropomorphism, but theomorphism. This is scientific. How else can you have vicarious knowledge?" *

* Pages 228-229.

If we have science it is an evidence or ground for belief in God. Conversely, to believe in God, implies and has bound up in it belief in science, in righteous government or sovereignty, and in justice. If we are agnostic as to God, logic demands that we be agnostic about everything, even physical appearances, and our nearest friends. Belief in God is the ground for belief in science and in our fellow men. Conversely, he who believes in men believes in God. Does not this give depth of meaning to the Scripture,—*Let not your heart by troubled; ye believe in God, believe also in me. Me* is not limited to Jesus but applies to prophets, apostles, martyrs, poets, artists, father and mother, brother and sister, husband and wife. Belief in God alone makes it possible really and deeply to believe in human relationships and alone gives meaning thereto.

"To sum up the question. If all calculation is simply fitting together data gained through the senses, namely, mental phenomena, in such a way that they are made to square with our thought processes and thus conform to the laws of mind, how would it be possibly by this process.

"(a) To get any knowledge at all of the external world, if it were not known to be the working of exactly the same infinite mind who is working through us, and therefore governed by the same laws?

*   *   *   *   *   *

"(b) How could we know the thought and intention of our friends unless they, too, were dependent on the same source and governed by the same laws? All this is saying that if we ever get outside of our present state of consciousness. that knowlege will be vicarious knowledge, and further that vicarious knowledge is an absurdity unless that which is outside is known to be uniform with that which is inside. There is absolutely no objective science, either physical or mental, unless from one, namely, the self, we can learn all. But if all are different in identity, distinct existences, there is no problem about it. It is simply impossible to have that knowledge, and there the matter ends.

"(c) And the same question comes up with regard to one's own personal identity, that is, his ability to connect his present experience with his past experience or to have a unity to his life. This can never be done by a dead lift of memory, but only through consciousness of objects, and through our ability to determine the changes through which they pass and the place into which our life fits. This takes us right back to the possibility of objective science again.

"(d) If a man's life is to fit into the life of others and become a part of one social order, so that his appointments are understood and followed by his friends, if history can have any significance to him, it will be because all others date and locate themselves and their plans in the same objective science which he has made the basis of his own personal identity. How could they work in the same way in which he works, get the same results that he gets, write history that he can read, literature that fills him with inspiration, enact laws that bind his conscience, unless they were dependent on the same source for their existence that nature and his own mind find working in themselves?

"(e) If we are to have a form of society which grants liberty, equality, and fraternity, it will only be on the basis of discussion. The ultimate appeal will be, not to force, but to evidence. This postulates that what is evidence to one mind is evidence to every mind when seen in connection with exactly the same data. How could you ever use the "therefore" in a syllogism unless, whether men willed it or not, they were obliged to assent to the conclusion when they had exactly your premises? They may be hasty, they may shut their eyes and refuse to see the matter at all, they may even persecute and ridicule, but you have an invincible ally in their own bosoms and they know it. They dare not allow themselves to think, for their whole nature will befriend you if you are right . . . When you discuss with a man it is simply because you yourself are within that man's inner life. You speak to the ear and he does not hear, but you speak to the heart from within and he cannot be deaf. Discussion is simply finding yourself in another, and that is the reason why you are courteous and respectful to others when you respect yourself. . . . If you are to have republican institutions, you must have faith in discussion. . . . If the majority have made a mistake, that mistake will be pointed out, and if they are in the right the truth will be more clear. The minority can submit when they know the justice of their cause is to be reviewed by the people, when they are convinced that the deepest, truest voice of the people is the voice of God Himself. This is arbitration, not war. This is liberty, equality, fraternity, not tyranny. This is monism, not pluralism.

"(f) What do we mean by freedom of the press? Not freedom to lie or to slander and misrepresent, but freedom to weigh evidence on the basis that when this is carefully done it will express the only verdict of each individual man who thinks the problem through and obtains the necessary data.

* * * * * *

"It is simply because men have no faith in reason, no love for the truth, that they question on the one hand the value of free discussions, and on the other hand become superstitious and servile imitators of society, asking not whether a thing is true, but whether it is good form . . . There is lack of moral sanitation, and absence of faith in humanity, when men cease to care for the truth supremely. Pluralism can have no other result, for then there could be no universal truth. Nothing would be possible for men except to imitate and become slaves. But monism clears the atmosphere of shame and reproach, falsehood and error, and gives all the dignity of God Himself to the truth.

* * * * * *

"(g) Freedom of our universities is a matter of considerable concern. It is often asked, 'Has not a man a right to do what he will with his own money? If he believes in a certain creed, and is willing to give a million dollars or ten million dollars to establish an institution to teach that creed, has he not a right to do it? . . . Have we not a right, then, to establish secretarian institutions?' On the basis of pluralism, most surely, but on the basis of monism, never. Look at it a moment. Has a man a right to form his own opinion arbitrarily, or only by the weighing of evidence? Well, then, if that is his duty, if his own conclusions must be shaped so as to square with the evidence, has he a right to do anything that would lead others to form their conclusions in a different way, to prevent them from weighing evidence, and make them borrow their results like a phonograph, that is, de-personalize them and take away the divine likeness with which God has endowed them? . . . There are two parts to our nature, brain paths and weighing evidence. The brain paths work along the lines of least resistance, and here force is the determining factor. But here man is only an animal. The human part of man is the power that can work in the lines of greatest resistance and square solely with evidence, and here man is in the image of God. Now whenever you substitute for evidence any form of force (and bribery is a form of force), you attempt murder, not of the body, but of the mind. You are doing what you can to do away with the spiritual and make man in the image of the beasts and birds and creeping things."*

The present writer would add another section or question. Has any church the right to adopt a creed and make nominal acceptance thereof a test for the clergy or for membership? Is not this the heresy of heresies? Is not this the reason above all others why churches today have so little power? How can a church have moral leadership when its very foundation is based upon immortality, namely, allegiance to authority or tradition, rather than to universal truth wherever found? Is this not the great evil of the present time, that the scientist, the business man, the lawyer, every department of life has more freedom and greater allegiance to the truth, than that which above all others should teach and preach in season and out of season freedom through the truth. The truth is the one guide of all our lives. If we own

---

* Pages 236-242.

supreme allegiance to church councils, to a book, to a
deified man, to tradition, to a creed, to any person or
thing except to the God of all truth, how can we justify
ourselves or expect to have power for righteousness?

Governing Motives: "In considering the motives and
standards of the moral life two alternatives present themselves; either pleasure is the only motive or there is a
spiritual nature and with it spiritual impulses; either
expediency is the only standard or this spiritual nature
and its constitution which involves justice and right is
the ultimate measure of value." ·

Our acts are ruled by governing motives.

"It will be found that there are only two commanders-
in-chief and that all our thoughtful actions report to one
of these·through whatever course of governing purposes.
It will be perceived that these supreme choices cannot
both govern action; if there is freedom it is here alone, it
is solely in the decision whether righteousness or selfishness shall be our supreme aim in existence." **

An important emphasis is to be laid on the doctrine
of selfness or self realization as the ultimate purpose of
life as opposed either to selfishness or to altruism. On
a pluralistic basis selfness and selfishness may seem synonymous but under monistic theism they are as different
as it is possible for two motives to be and selfness becomes synonymous with righteousness.

"Some day I hope to make the world 'realize' as well
as know these two things: (a) that we 'judge', 'feel',
and 'will' for nature and our fellow-men vicariously,
and must; (b) that it is absurd to make ourselves the

---

* Pages 51-52.
** Page 263.

standard for others and for nature, if we are distinct beings who may have entirely different constitutions.

"It is a large task, but it simply means waking people up, and making them observe what they are doing all the time when they study science, or sit on the jury, or criticise their neighbor. When I have done this, the question begins to be vital as to what this 'constitution,' identical in every man and everything, and revealed so clearly in our own consciousness, is striving to realize in this world of objects. Either the question is insoluble, absolutely so. or the answer must come as to all others, viz., vicariously, by the study of self. Either God is not revealed at all and can never be, or He can be known through the workings of our own inner life. Theism proves that we are partakers of the divine nature, made in His image: so in knowing the deepest truth of our own being, we discover the laws that hold of Him. We are more sure of our knowledge of God than of our knowledge of nature or of man, for if these truths concerning ourselves do not hold of Him, how can we know them to hold of things and beings outside of and apart from us? e. g., we are more sure of the truths of space than we are of the planets, for how know them if geometry is false? When we begin to seek a solution of the 'riddle of the universe' by the only process open to us, we come directly to the answer given in Scripture, 'Not for your sakes, O house of Israel, but for mine own name's sake have I done this.' Self-realization is the ultimate impulse of self; not merely to exist, but to exist in the fullness of one's power, in the completeness of life which is the perfection of (1) self-consciousness, (2) self-direction and control, and, (3) self-appreciation and valuation. This alone is personality. The self is ever striving for true personal existence." *

"The next question is, How is self-realization for God and men possible? . . . 'Consciousness of self or subject is possible only through consciousness of objects. A worldless God is as impossible as a Godless world.' Perfection of self-consciousness is possible only through unity and identity of objects. . . . Hence if God is to be eternally self-conscious, then some of his objects must be immortal. 'Because I live, ye shall live also.'" **

"If perfection of self is possible only through perfection of objects, then the universe must be perfect or God is not. This is the problem of evil. I can only outline the investigation. The physical world is not complete, but it is perfect in the sense that there is no violation of law. There has never been a moment when it has failed to obey in every part. Hence when first created it was 'all very good.' But God could not create man perfect, since human perfection must be man's own achievement or it is nothing. . . . Moral right must be the man's own act, and he cannot have the power to do moral right unless he has the power also to do wrong. Either God must not create man at all, or He must create him in His own image, and give him power of choice. God must then persuade, educate, assist; He cannot compel a right act on man's part. If God has made a universe that does all that can be done to persuade, educate and assist, then when evil comes the blame is on man.

"This is clear enough in some cases but not in others. The question is one of fact, not of principle. Is every-

* Pages 114-115.
** Page 116.

thing that infinite wisdom and love could devise done
to influence men to do right? Surely not, for we can
think of many things that would have diminished particular evils. But here we are met with the question, Is
the 'lack' the fault of God or of man?" *

For further discussion see the volume referred to.

"But what are we to do with the cruelty in nature,
such as volcanoes, sickness, and the like?

"Must we not here consider process rather than product, as for example, in railroading we admire the process
of transportation, even if great disaster comes when
through ignorance it is wrongly used. If God has created
chemical elements and physical forces that, when used cor-
rectly, constitute a universe exactly fitted for a society
of human beings inspired by the highest virtue, then when
men are ignorant and selfish and fail so to use nature we
cannot blame nature. Electricity left wild in nature is
the thunderbolt, but used by science it is the telegraph,
trolley, electric light, and a thousand other things; so
we do not condemn electricity because of thunderstorms.
More than that, man (the race) by learning how to use it
properly attains self-development, lifts himself to the
highest level, and becomes co-creator with God in making
a beautiful world. . . . God would be a poor teacher
if He did not allow His pupils to depend largely on themselves for the answer to their problems. . . .

"Here, then, is another question which we can answer
here and there; the full reply can come only when science
has done its utmost in mastering the forces of nature.
Possibly, then, physical evils can either be controlled or

---

* Pages 116-117.

predicted and avoided. Volcanoes are products; the processes are those chemical and physical ones familiar to our daily life, and, rightly used, of infinite worth to man; not for a moment could we consent to have steam lose its power. Already science has discovered much good from volcanoes and done something to discover their laws so as to give ground for hope that some day we shall know much more. Should the time come when their activity can be anticipated they would work good and the harm could be avoided." ⁚

"You see I have tried to state the question, not to answer it. . . . We must not consider nature as a whole but only as a part, and man as the other factor. Perfection is in neither alone, but only comes when each is doing its full share. Nature is never behind man's intelligence; when he is aroused to explore, nature is there to reveal her secret. God sees the end from the beginning; only when man can so view it can he substitute sight for faith. Faith, then, has a distinct sphere. Not to take the place of evidence when considering the problem of God's existence, His nature or His personality; those are questions for philosophy. But if these are solved, if we know Him, then we turn to considering His work. Is it perfect or is it wrong, and does it not reveal neglect and defect in His moral character? Here is the sphere of faith. While the building is being constructed, the onlooker cannot see beauty in the ugly piles of stones and timber. Yet if he knows the architect directly he may have faith (he cannot have sight) that each stone is best suited to its place in the grand whole, and that the temple when finished

---

* Pages 120-121.

will have no flaw. But this faith must rest on knowledge of the person back of it all." *

It has already been stated that there are only two supreme governing motives, selfishness and righteousness. But what is righteousness? Self-realization, selfness, has been mentioned as synonymous, on a monistic theistic basis, with righteousness. What is selfness? Many persons appear to miss the essential difference between altruism or seeking the happiness of others and righteousness.

As to altruism, Professor Garman said,

"I can only find two answers possible here. (1) The thought of others' enjoyment may be a source of greater pleasure to him than those pleasures he has sacrificed. . . . Such altruism would be no altruism at all— only shrewd selfishness. (2) That there is some other standard of conduct than pleasure. Christ, for instance, did not consider what He was to gain or lose by His career any more than an auditor of a bank, when he follows the multiplication table, is looking for a reward. He figures 'five times five are twenty-five,' not because that number will give him more happiness than either a higher or a lower one, but simply because it is the truth. Why may not truth (justice) be as ultimate for the will as for the intellect? If so, process not product would be our standard in ethics as truly as in mathematics.

"But, you ask, is not a third position possible, viz., unselfishness, or the welfare of others? May not one bear a surplus of suffering just for the sake of benefiting the

---

* Page 122.

race, i.e., for the greatest good to the greatest number?" *

"This is a commercial age, and mere quantity is everything to some minds. 'Greatest good to the greatest number' implies to them that mere numbers introduce some new factor into the problem of conduct. What answer can be made to these persons? . . . There can be no doubt of their sincerity. It is true that in some spheres difference in degree or mere magnitude makes a difference of kind in results attained. For instance: under fourteen vibrations a second the ear detects only separate noises, but above that number we may get a musical note. At a given temperature plants grow and blossom; diminish the heat sufficiently and they are killed by frost. It is one thing to talk with an individual acquaintance, but quite another to address a large audience. A chemist is satisfied with a small bottle of sea water for analysis, since he thereby determines the composition of the ocean itself. But if the whole of Neptune's kingdom were put in bottles, and the Wandering Jew should live long enough to examine each one singly, he would have seen no ocean, no ebb and flow of tides, no dashing of breakers, no earthquake waves. Mere quantity is a vital matter. This is especially true in monetary affairs, and it is not strange that a commercial age jumps to the conclusion that it is everything in ethics. But if you look not at results, but at processes, the case is different. Tyndall tells us 'where law is concerned there is no great and no small. The force that moulds the tear rounds the planet.' Gravity can be tested as truly by the pendulum as by a whole

---

* Page 283.

heaven full of stars. In ethics we are concerned with processes." *

"Looking not at products but at processes, good to one is good to and for all; the greatest good to one is the greatest good, the only ultimate good, to every one, not simply to the majority.

"It is a mistake to affirm that the happiness of the community is so much greater than that of individuals; that they should. therefore. be sacrificed for the good of the whole. There is no such thing as happiness of the community. . . . Springs of water may mingle their overflow and make a brook, brooks may empty into each other and produce a river, then all rivers flow into the ocean and become part of one vast aggregate of waters; but this never happens in the personal life of individuals. The community, as the term is here used, is composed of individuals in relationship, therefore the happiness of the whole can never be greater in degree than the happiness of the most favored individual therein." **

"Now that we are on the subject of altruism, I must say a word as to its essential immorality (when taken in the sense of making one's self 'merely a means' to others' happiness). The term surprises you, but it is not a whit too strong. If it is possible to put self and its welfare completely out of sight in order to labor solely for others, it will be equally possible to put out of sight self and its responsibilities and obligations. Unless self is the centre of one's horizon and is degraded by wrong doing and ennobled by right doing, there is nothing to tie to, nothing to bind the person to the path of duty.

---

* Pages 287-288.
** Page 288.

Life becomes impersonal. *merely a means to an end and never an end in itself;* hence a mere thing to be used or abused by others. Now this is exactly the principle of bossism. The boss and the tyrant alone have personality; all their followers are simply tools to be used as they please. . . . You know what this self-abnegation has meant in religious history. Freedom of scientific thought, right of private interpretation of Scripture, conscience, friendships the most sacred, all have been offered up at the command of the Church." *

"Only two supreme choices are conceivable when we think concretely. Either one must be supremely selfish, make his own happiness the end of his existence and sacrifice temporary advantages for others' welfare only as a way of getting greater pleasure or of avoiding something unpleasant, or he must drop out happiness altogether *as an end,* not merely his own, but that of others and even of the race. It may be a means, a by-product, just as truly as health or wealth; therefore it may be even a duty to strive for it when conditions make it an effective means. . . . But it must always be valued at its true worth, and one cannot be too careful to avoid the mistake of the miser who makes the means the end." **

Righteousness, right action, requires or rather involves assistance of right wherever found and resistance of wrong. As finite beings our powers are limited, and there is also the question of means or how we shall assist or resist. The questions that now confront us are the principles of sovereignty, and also how to resist wrong doing or the general theories of punishment or justice.

---

* Page 289.
** Pages 290-291.

"Out work in ethics is divided into two subdivisions: first, subjective ethics, which deals with the motive of the true ethical life; secondly, objective ethics, which deals with the processes of the ethical life as it realizes itself in actual existence. We begin with the doctrine of the State and show that actual life is impossible apart from relationships. Then we go on to show that man has no dual personality; he is not endowed with two minds, the one to be used in the sphere of religion and the other in the sphere of government and society; that man is always and everywhere himself; that he has but one set of principles by which to guide his conduct; that love to God and love to man are, from the point of view of the finite, exactly the same process. From this point of view it is impossible to take up the study of objective ethics at all without covering the sphere of the State and of society. We make, therefore, the study of political obligations the very basis of our work. We attempt to show that as gravitation acts according to the same law, whether in the case of a planet or in the case of a pendulum, so man has exactly the same standard of obligation and the same principles of ethical judgment in dealing with human affairs that he has in dealing with God. If the powers that be are all ordained of God, then the law which governs these must be divine. We throw our whole weight on the doctrine that there is no such thing as political ethics apart from divine ethics, and any attempt so to consider human life is an abandonment of ethics altogether to mere calculations of expediency." *

"The common view makes the individual first and re-

---

* Page 99.

lationships secondary. Of course this is so. How could there be a relationship unless there were some things to be related? No relationship is necessary; surely not that involved in sovereignty. If you hold these premises, only one motive can influence the individual, and that is expediency. Liberty, equality, fraternity are simply forms of courtesy; they mean nothing. When it comes to the test, self-preference is the ultimate motive. . . . Might makes right. There is, therefore, no mean between anarchy and tyranny. The successful man is the tyrant, the under dog in the fight is the anarchist. This is the last word on all governmental and social problems the moment you tell the truth. It is not expedient to do so always. Might includes trick and diplomacy and shrewdness, yes, and lying too, quite as much as physical power.

"The theistic view is a startling paradox. It affirms that the relationship is first and that the individual is its product. This is all of the subject the common man will care to know. Such a view is moonshine, a mere theory. Wit is a discoverer of incongruities of a certain type, and nothing is more incongruous with the common view than this doctrine. From the days of Plato to the present time it has been a fair target for ridicule. But let us look at the facts. If man is a dependent being, his relationship to God is that which gives him existence. . . . Secondly, if all other things are dependent on God. they necessarily determine each other."*

"Take our physical life. Does a man first exist and then come into certain relationships? Take those of the

* Pages 323-324.

physical world, e.g., that of gravitation. Does a man at a definite time in his life conclude to submit himself to this particular law, or must gravitation be first, in order for the man to exist at all? Suspend gravitation for a moment and what would happen to him? Not a particle of atmosphere would enter his lungs, all the finer blood-vessels would instantly burst when the pressure was removed, and the rotation of the earth would whirl him off in a tangent into empty space at the rate of a thousand miles an hour. Take those relationships that are expressed by chemical affinity. Suspend these and what would become of nutrition, and how long would a man exist if there was no chemical action at all in his physical frame? Suspend the law of cause and effect and what could man do for himself? When he put out his foot to walk the ground would offer no resistance. When he sat down the chair would give him no support. When he turned his eyes towards the sun it would give him no sensations of sight. Neither could he have hearing, touch, taste, or smell. When we say that these relationships are first we mean logically rather than chronologically. Chronologically they are simultaneous, as cause and effect always are. If a cause ceased to exist before the effect came into being, then this would be an event without a cause."*

"Let us discuss mental relations. Most people think personality is as a unity, just like gold; that one is passively personal, therefore one could act as a personal being even if everything in the world were annihilated. But this is superficial. Personality is always an achieve-

---

* Page 325.

ment, not gained once for all, but requiring infinite repetition. A personal being is simply a conscious being whose consciousness has reached the grade in which it knows itself. But power reveals itself only in work done. If the self did nothing, it could not be self-conscious. The grade of self-consciousness is determined, then, by the amount the self does, not once for all, way back in the past, but continually. Hence our personality is fluctuating with our activity. When an orator outdoes himself he rises to a very high level of personality; when he fails he sinks pretty low in his own estimation. Now there are only three kinds of activity possible; knowing or thinking, feeling, and willing. Let us take thinking, since we cannot very well will or feel until we know. You cannot think without thinking about something, either objects about you or ideas that you originate. If you have no objects in nature or in imagination, then you have no thought, no personality. This is what is meant by the statement 'Consciousness of subject is possible only through consciousness of object.' One step more. Imagination is not really creative. A blind man cannot create color; a man born deaf cannot create sound. Unless in childhood nature actually existed and related herself to us in a causal way, producing sensations in us as our earliest objects, we never could have begun the personal life. Here we are, then. Relationship, is logically first and personality is its product."*

"It is the contact of mind with mind that is the only condition of a human life. This is only saying that the perfection of the subject depends upon the perfection of

---

* Page 326.

its objects. Our social relations, including family relations, are first, and sanity is the product. We consider it a personal loss when our friends die; it takes away just so much of our personality. Here, then, is the great fact concerning our existence. In no instance can we free ourselves from the law that the relationship is first and we are the product, and our life continues only so long as the relationship continues. This is the formula: A determines B and B determines A; that is A never determines himself directly, but only through B. If you walk you act upon the ground, it reacts, giving you support, and you move forward. . . . We are inspired and lifted up by our contact with each other. It will be seen, then, that the whole is very different from an aggregation of parts. The civil compact theory affirms that because one man has no prerogative over another, society can have no prerogative over the individual, because society is made up of individuals and the whole cannot be greater than the sum of the parts. Nothing is more ridiculous than this system. . . . Society is not composed of individuals; society is a relationship by virtue of which individuals come into existence and without which they would have no being as personal." *

"We may now ask: What is this relationship which constitutes sovereignty, and how is it that on our new premises sovereignty does not de-personalize the individual? Sovereignty is a particular relationship which is not created by man and which he cannot divest himself of. By virtue of this relationship only does he become personal. Let us see if we can find this particular relationship.

---

* Pages 327-328.

Suppose an ocean liner trying to break its record. When passing the Newfoundland banks it discovers a shipwreck-ed sailor afloat on a spar a half mile off. All eyes see him and bring him to the notice of the captain. What of it? An interesting sight. no doubt, gives them something to talk about and breaks up the tedium of the voyage. That sailor is a foreigner. What do people on that steamer care for him or his life? And yet their knowledge of his situation makes it impossible for them to go on their way and leave him there without becoming murderers. Here is the simple law. Man is so constituted that there is a peculiar relationship between his intellect and his will, and when he knows, he is obliged to act. How he acts is decided by the will if it is free, but the will cannot decide whether it will act or not under such conditions as are now present. That ship captain has got to stop his vessel, lose his record. and save that sailor, or be a murderer. He may care as little as he pleases for the sailor, but if he cares for his own moral character he will stop that ship. This is not a matter of his choosing. He abominates the whole predicament. But there he is, and he has only one question before him, How will he act? Take another case. A policeman standing on the corner of a street in the rough part of a city sees a scoundrel assault a woman who makes desperate resis-tance. The moment the policeman knows what is going on, he, too, must act. If he stands there and renders no assistance, he is an accomplice of the criminal, aiding and abetting him in his crime, that is, he too. becomes crim-inal. He may regret extremely the necessity that is upon him, but he cannot escape by doing nothing. In some way he must act, and the only question is, How. If the ship captain or the policeman had not known what was going on, the dilemma would not have arisen, but the moment knowledge comes, sovereignty begins. We may see this more clearly in the case of the assassination of Lincoln. When Booth had made his escape any man who recognized and failed to report him was considered as his accomplice, aiding and abetting Booth and resisting the government. Such an accomplice was liable to the extreme penalty of the law. See how embarrassing was the position. If a person had not recognized him, had not known anything about the crime, there would have been no occasion for action. But when circumstances placed the individual where he had the knowledge, then he entered into a new life; either he became a criminal himself or he became an avenger of the martyred President. No longer could he be inactive. This is the penalty he pays for being personal. To be personal is to be sovereign. When circumstances conspire to bring a matter into the sphere of our knowledge, then we have to interfere, either in the line of aiding and abetting or in that of resisting. This is the only sovereignty that can exist consistently with personality. The question of how we shall aid or how we shall resist is wholly a question of means. We may do it in an organized form and then we shall have government, or we may do so without a form of organization and then we have simply society, but in both cases we have sovereignty."*

"Sovereignty, we may say, then, is the interference of one individual with the affairs of another individual, either in the line of resisting or in that of assisting. You

---

* Pages 328-330.

will see that it does not depend upon any compact any more than the attraction of the earth by the sun depends upon compact. You see that it is only a form of that relationship of cause and effect by virtue of which personal life is possible. Sovereignty simply postulates that the mind is a cause in the universe as truly as matter, the only difference being, matter can work automatically without intelligence, mind can work only when it is intelligent. Matter can act only one way, that is, it is fated. Mind can work either rightly or wrongly, if you have free will. But when a man does wrong he interferes with his fellow-man and exercises sovereignty as truly as when he does right, unless you please to define sovereignty as right interference, and tyranny as wrong interference. It seems to be better, however, to speak of sovereignty as interference. Human sovereignty has limits, but they are simply limits of knowledge and ability. Our ability is much more limited than our knowledge. Many things which we know about we have not strength enough to remedy; hence we aid and abet them unwillingly. Other things we are not skillful enough to remedy, but should do greater evil if we attempted it. The ordinary man is not skillful enough to perform an operation upon appendicitis, and if, on a hnuting tour, he is with his friend who is taken ill in this way, he would have to allow him to die a natural death rather than to torture him to death by a bungling operation. These are simply the limitations of finiteness. They do not exist with God, who is the ideal sovereign, and who cannot know human deeds without interfering either in the line of aiding or in that of resisting them." *

---

* Pages 330-331.

Before considering the method of divine sovereignty let us consider the sphere or realm of human sovereignty.

"It is a general law of all mental life that consciousness of self is possible only through consciousness of objects. A similar law holds in moral life and the social order. We may state this in the formula, A determines himself never directly, but always through B, i.e., a man determines his character and personality by the attitude and relations he assumes towards his world of nature and persons.

"If A determines himself through B, then there are only four possible spheres of life for A, due to the four possible conditions of B . . .

1. B may be strong and do right.
2. B may be strong and do wrong.
3. B may be weak and do right.
4. B may be weak and do wrong.

Every phase of life comes in here.

(1) is the sphere of business, where action and reaction should be equal; (2) is the sphere of punishment, where the action must take the form of resistance to the wrongdoer; (3) is the sphere of charity, where the strong must help the weak; (4) is the sphere for the atonement, where the strong must resist by assistance."*

"Business is the action and reaction in the state under conditions of equality. The law is that each person engaged in the transaction must be both means and end. This occurs only when the service rendered is an equivalent for the service received. This is justice.
Observe that such a transaction under the conditions is as

---

* Page 322.

truly a *"labor of love,"* that is, as truly conforms to the requirements of the organic unity, as charity and martyrdom under different conditions."*

"Charity is the action and reaction that takes place in the state under conditions of relative inequality on the part of those engaged. It is a condition of a diseased organism. The law of charity is that, for the time being, the strong shall help the weak without recompense, i.e., shall be means, not end, until the condition of health is restored. If the hand is diseased the body must heal it, and, in the mean time, give it rest. This may be a severer test, but is no more a labor of love than is business. Charity under conditions of relative equality is as truly a crime as dishonesty. 2 Thess. 3: 10: 'For even, when we were with you. this we commanded you. that if any would not work neither should he eat' "**

How resist the evil doer when he is strong?

"In studying punishment we are studying the principle of authority, just as Newton studied the apple and found the laws of science."†

There have been five principal theories of punishment:‡

(1) Vengeance:

This makes punishment depend upon human passion and opens the door for all kinds of pain.

(2) Retribution:

"We have a phrase that a person 'paid the debt', or that he 'ought to have suffered'. Taken

---

* Page 336.
** Pages 336-337.
† Page 315.
‡ See pages 315 and following; also based upon classroom notes taken by the present writer.

literally what does it mean? If you pay the debt, there has been an exchange. Some of the consequences may be undone, and some may not. But if the idea is to right a wrong which has been committed it is useless, because the wrong, considered as a moral deed, cannot be undone. . . Two wrongs can never make a right. Why should this individual be made to suffer because he has made others suffer?"

(3) Pathological:

Is all sin simply disease needing only removal of some physical cause? This theory is contrary to all that has gone before in this chapter so it is not considered that there is need of repetition at this time.

(4) Reformation:

"Is punishment to reform? Then the criminal would put the state under obligation to do the best for his health, and this might be to send him to Europe and give him an education." Besides this theory comes back to altruism, already reviewed critically.

(5) Prevention:

"Is punishment to prevent a man from doing a deed again? We kill a man for committing a murder; then why didn't we kill him before he commited the murder? Cannot you go down into the slums of New York and pick out the men who would commit murder if they had the chance? . . . Now who is there in the whole crowd that, under temptation enough, wouldn't be a dangerous person to have around? When the woman taken in adultery was brought to Jesus, . . . 'He that is without sin among you, let him first cast a stone at her.' And then they began to think that if they were enough tempted they wouldn't be quite safe, and they skulked out, from the greatest to the least. And yet we hear over and over again that punishment is to protect the state. That may be an effect of it, as the growing of the grass is an effect of the shining of the sun. We are after the *nature* of punishment now."

Or if not to prevent a particular individual from committing a crime,—"May not punishment be to prevent others from committing crime? We will make an example of the criminal. Once in English history a judge sentenced a man for stealing sheep. The judge said: 'You are not punished because *you* steal sheep, but in order that sheep may not be stolen.' The reply was, 'What's that to me, sir?' Gentlemen, where you make one suffer for the wrong of another, do you call that punishment or martyrdom? Is that justice or injustice? The criminal may say: If others were not so frail and and so weak, I should not have to suffer."

"You say you have got to have punishment, or the state will go to smash. But is it *right?* If we hold that might is right, then we are Nihilists. Similarly, God's authority has generally been taken on the principle that might makes right,

but if it does with God, it does with us. If
we are Nihilists, let us say so right out."*

(6) "We now have a sixth theory for punishment.
Why do we punish the criminal? The reply is, We never
punish the deed but only the doer. We punish only when
we cannot help acting, when we are obliged to assist or resist the criminal. Punishment is the resistance of the
wrongdoer. Assistance to the right doer is the reward.
Now why do we punish? Not for the sake of vengeance, or reformation, or retribution, or prevention, in the
historic meaning of that word, but simply for our own
sake. If we are in such circumstances that we must act,
we will act rightly, whether others do or not. . . If
others do wrong there is no reason why we should when
we are forced to act. The Spartans at Thermopylae won
the admiration of history, not because their defense was
successful, but because they died game. They would do
nothing to aid the invaders of their land. . . Even the
newsboy has no respect for his mates when they fail to insist upon their own honor by resenting degrading treatment from another. This is punishment; because
when you are forced to act, if you act rightly while the
person on whom you act is acting wrongly, there will be a
collision, and pain inflicted as a result of sovereignty. But
you see that is it not vicarious. Others indeed may take
warning and not collide with us. But that is a by-product.
If there was only one transgressor in the universe and
we were so situated that we could not avoid assisting
or resisting him, we should be under just as much obligation as though every one were an evil doer. Our sole

---

* Page 317.

motive, if righteous, would be not to cause him to suffer, but to prevent becoming criminal ourselves. The converse is true also. Why do we reward good conduct? . . . All noble-minded people feel that they degrade themselves when they do not render 'honor to whom honor is due.' . . . The person who has no respect for himself cannot be relied upon to be courteous towards others. It is seen, therefore, that sovereignty is a very much broader term than government. Government is only a very particular administration of sovereignty under certain conditions." *

"To worship is to become conscious of the worth of the Divine Being."**

There yet remains to be considered action when B may be weak and do wrong, "the sphere for the atonement where the strong must resist by assistance."†

The method of resistance is dependent upon circumstances. When B is strong, he must be opposed to the full extent of our powers. Sometimes it is necessary for us to use all the powers at our command including physical force to the limit.

But when we realize our obligation, not as a matter of choice but of stern duty, always to assist the right and resist the wrong, we are overwhelmed, and feel who is sufficient for these things. So often do we fail, that if God, all powerful, did resist us to the limit, we would be annihilated. But the divine method of resisting evil is resistance through assistance. This is the method of at-one-ment. Justice and mercy become synonymous. There

* Pages 331-333.
** From classroom note taken by the writer.
† Page 322.

is hope for the evil doer, through acceptance of divine aid, and making supreme choice of righteousness as the motive for his own life.

By the atonement, the present writer does not mean vicarious punishment of Jesus for the sins of the world, nor is it to be understood as one distinct and historic event. Rather the atonement is a continuous atonement, the divine method of resisting evil through mercy and love. And as this is the method of God so it should be the method of us all. There is not one method for God, another for man. Inasmuch as we partake of the divine nature, we are to follow the divine method as far as possible for us in our finiteness. "The divine method is one of mercy which makes possible repentance and at-one-ment."*

"Let me just here . . . call attention to the possible extremes of view to be found in the history of human progress. The narrowest idea conceivable is that of fetichism, where each object is an entity by itself, and, in addition, all the more common attributes are personified into independent beings. The other extreme is theism (than which a broader, grander idea of the universe is impossible); it is this: God or Spirit is the only independent reality, and any other being or event is but a dependent 'phase', or 'state' or 'product' of His activity. He is 'the all in all'. 'In Him all things live and move and have their being.' He is the Hebrew Jehovah, the 'I AM', the self-existent and eternal One who filleth immensity and inhabiteth eternity. The Ancient of Days, in terms of whose action Time itself is measured. Nature

---

* From classroom notes taken by the writer.

is related to God as 'thought to the mind that thinks', as 'music to the air that is in vibration', as 'light to the ether'. Nature is the 'living garment of God', that is, the continued activity in which He manifests Himself. Between these extremes would lie (1) The successive phases of Polytheism. These eventually lead to (2) Materialism, where science begins in its atomic form. The progress of science would make necessary at length (3) Dualism, or the doctrine that there are two independent entities, mind and matter; at this stage all the conflicts between science and religion arise. But this must, sooner or later, be resolved into the last and final position of philosophy, viz., (4) Theism as above explained." *

"If we look back over the history of human thinking, we find these stages clearly marked. The first great era was occupied with the problem, 'What is nature?' In prehistoric times men were afraid of nature; it was their enemy, the hiding-place of ghosts and hobgoblins and malicious spirits who were bent on doing men harm. The first era of philosophic thought worked out the mechanical conception of nature and taught man that it was neither friend nor foe, but simply his tool, to be used with skill instead of ignorance. The modern atomic theory was originated by Democritus; the theory of evolution was crudely formulated by Empedocles, and most of our modern scientific conceptions had some prototype in this early stage of Greek reflection. This was a wonderful step in progress, and the world has never been quite the same as it was before. You know how it is with the century plant. It lives and grows, but generations come and

---

* Pages 247-248.

go before it blossoms. Science is not a century plant, but a plant of millenniums. It took root in this earliest day of Greek thinking, but two thousand years passed away before it blossomed. We today see the beauty of the flower."*

"The next great problem was, 'What is man?' Before this question was asked he was a nobody. The state was everything, the individual nothing. But under the influence of the sophists, of Socrates, Plato, and Aristotle, the worth of man as an individual began to be revealed. Even Meno's slave was found to possess a divine nature that made him a peer of those who had despised him. The worth of man as man, his power to know truth that had before seemed only the prerogative of the gods to know, arrested attention. There was no longer 'Greek nor Jew, Barbarian, Scythian, bond nor free', but mind was all and in all. In the breaking up of Greek political life, in the loss of their material splendor, when their national sun had set, the stars of the spiritual firmament began to shine and all the wise men wondered."**

"The next question was, 'What is God?' And as the more advanced and candid thought on this question they gradually gave up their polytheism and their pluralism and came out squarely on the monistic basis. Stoicism was through and through monistic."†

The long line of the great Hebrew religious leaders and prophets with their monotheism and belief in the unity and righteousness of God culminated in Jesus. He "taught

---

* Page 379.
** Pages 379-380.
† Page 380.

the Fatherhood of God and the doctrine of the atonement."*

"The fourth great question was, 'The problem of evil'. Here we have the great Augustinian controversies. It was a period of decay; the corruption of the Roman Empire was everywhere revolting. The beginning of the night of the Middle Ages brought a return from the monistic conception back again to pluralism. First, because on this basis it seemed so much easier to explain evil; and secondly, because the barbarians could more easily understand pluralism, whereas monism was hard to grasp."**

"The fifth question was, 'How can sinful man be just with God?' This was the time of the Protestant Reformation, and it brought out the problem of justification by faith, the forgiveness of sins through repentance. It formulated the doctrine of the atonement as vicarious—vicarious punishment."†

"The sixth question was, 'How shall man be just with his sinful fellow-man' . . . You remember one scene in Christ's life where he went up into the mountain and. while there, was transfigured; his disciples saw him no longer a man of sorrows acquainted with grief, but in his divine grandeur, and with him Moses, who represented the law that he fulfilled, and Elias, who represented the prophecies which he had brought to pass. It seems to me that philosophy is the mount of transfiguration of human nature, and that if we study it rightly we no longer see only that which is base and mean and selfish and slavish, which actual life makes so much of, but we

* Page 380.
** Page 380.
† Pages 380-381.

have revealed to us the divine spirit which is working out through it all. Then we discover that this side of human life alone gives meaning to science, which stands for law in modern times, and to society, which has ever looked forward to a future beyond the power of mere man to realize. Industrial life, which has been so often condemned as having nothing but selfishness in it, is seen to be a reincarnation of the divine in human character; for it is nothing but sovereignty on its positive side, where the strong make the service given an equivalent for the service received in business, and in charity the strong help the weak to become strong and thus help themselves. . . . And man will adopt the same schemes for resisting the sins of his fellow-man that God has adopted for resisting the sin of the world. Then man will not merely think God's thought after Him in physical science, but he will live God's life after Him in his social existence."*

"This is a new way of looking at things, and it requires something besides thinking to take this view. No one can follow truth without being an actual hero, for the multitude do not go that way; they follow custom. Remember the experience of Columbus when he dared to live up to the evidence which proved to him that the world was round. Derided by his contemporaries, he steered his ships towards the west with nothing to guide him except the great truths which science had revealed. Was the courage of that man a small achievement? To be a hero in battle is merely to follow the footsteps of a great

---

* Pages 381-382. (Note: In those pages personal pronouns referring to Christ are capitalized. I have used capitals only when pronouns refer to God.)

company of patriots who fairly blaze with glory. But to be alone on an unknown sea, where the very laws of nature seem to be changing and the most trusted friends call you crazy, and then to dare every peril, inspired by the faith in the unseen country, is sublime. Let this be a prophecy for your life. The old country from which you set sail on your voyage of life is the material shore. It is the kingdom of brain paths, where selfishness is not sovereign, but tyrant. It is the prevailing view of the citizens of this country, that there is no other land. We have given evidence to show that there is a Western hemisphere, a spiritual America, the home of freedom, a commonwealth whose inhabitants are citizens of the kingdom of Truth, whose achievements constitute all that is grand and heroic in human life. I beg you to follow Columbus. You will be ridiculed for your faith as he was for his. But refuse to deal with men simply as selfish beings. If your efforts seem to come to naught, and even those who are your helpers beg you to give up the voyage and turn back, push boldly on towards the other shore. If your heart does not fail, there will come a time when you shall have passed the fogs of doubt, weathered the storms of ridicule, and at last made a harbor in the spiritual life of humanity."*

* Pages 384-385.

CHAPTER XII

This little book does not profess to be a systematic presentation of theology, but only an introduction to the subject.

The writer fully recognizes that in method and in statements as well as in conclusions, it differs fundamentally both from the commonly accepted conservative belief and from the liberal theological position of the present time. For its denials no school or no individual is in any sense whatsoever responsible except the writer.

It is admitted that the positions stated, both affirmative and negative, are so absolutely at variance with any type of Christian theology, Roman Catholic, Protestant or Modernist, that any one who thoroughly accepts them, will probably never more call himself a Christian or wish to remain in the Christian church, or be willing to repeat the creeds, whether Apostles', Nicene, or Athanasian, no matter how interpreted or with what reservations soever. Too often at present the question is how repeat or how use the ancient symbols with mental reservations or reading into them new meanings. This is the bane of theology and the church. Better by far are erroneous statements, believed and stated unequivocally, than fine distinctions of meaning so hedged about with reservations and so interpreted that none understand what is really meant. Clarity of statment is essential to clarity of thought and is the way to the truth.

The writer has never forgotten an experience of his

own seminary days. After two years at Yale he felt that perhaps he had arrived at the Unitarian position and went to Cambridge to consult concerning the advisibity of finishing his course at Harvard Divinity School, where the faculty was for the most part nominally Unitarian. By the member of that faculty consulted, he was advised to finish his course at Yale. This was most excellent advice, which he has ever since been glad that he followed, because it is never well to avoid a direct issue where one is. The reason given with the advice, however, was that it was unwise to change because the teaching of the two schools was practically the same. This was a tremendous shock. The writer then felt that Unitarianism should be a realm of freedom and affirmation, as far removed from Protestantism as the latter must have seemed from Roman Catholicism in the sixteenth century. Modern liberal theology seems, generally speaking, to be only more negative than liberal orthodoxy, or if perchance it does become affirmative, too often runs into vagaries of social and economic radicalism.

The truth is at once very conservative and very progressive. "Sooner could I doubt my own existence than think that Truth is not." Augustine.

While we do not attempt to deny or to make little of differences between the theology outlined in this little book, and that to which in the past we have been accustomed, there is a continuity, indeed a basic oneness. It is simply that we have in the past been troubled about many non-essentials and tried to hold to them amid growing difficulties. They may seem essential but are not.

Probably no Christian doctrine is believed to be more vital than belief in the divine incarnation in Christ, and in his unique and sole divinity. But is not this a non-essential doctrine, in fact does not denial of the unique and sole sonship of Jesus become necessary if we are to refuse to deny, and if we hold to, belief in the present incarnation of God in every human soul.

Doubt and denial of accepted beliefs has too often been made synonymous with doubt and denial of religion and of the religious view of the world and of human relations. In reality the hiding of doubts usually results first in self-deception, and then in deception of others. Doubts and unbeliefs courageously expressed, not in a contentious or an argumentative way, but in honest sincerity, lead to larger outlook and end in positive beliefs. The biographies of individual thinkers and the history of philosophy and of theology abundantly prove this.

In any event, of this we are sure. No church and no theologian, that refuses to meet all sincere questions and doubts and freely and in a straight-forward manner consider and answer them, is worthy of the allegiance or the respect of an honest man or woman.

One of the main purposes of this little book is to show that if once we cease trying to convince ourselves of that which we have been taught ought to be believed, but which we do not deeply believe, the whole problem is illuminated and we begin to catch a glimpse of profound realities which, if once seen, will evermore hold our allegiance because we cannot believe or act otherwise.

At present there is a wide-spread tendency to decry theology and to try to substitute therefor sociology and psychology, forgetting that a fundamental question is whether or not we have any science at all. This is a metaphysical problem. Unless we do have vicarious knowledge why trouble about any sciences, and if we do have it, then theology becomes central.

It may be said that one does not have to understand theology to live a religious life. Neither does one have to understand or even know the scientific laws of gravitation to conduct his physical life. Yet as a study of physics has led to wonderful development in the physical realm so will study of theology broaden and deepen the religious life.

The method of theology must be that of freedom, and supreme allegiance to the truth. The processes are scientific. The aim and object is clearer knowledge of God and man, and of the relation of man to God, and to his fellow-men, to the end that life may be lived in the strength and to the praise and glory of God, which is manifest in the life that now is.

"Henry George's familiar story of the child who was surprised to find that her father's garden was part of that surface of the earth of which she was studying in her geography class, is paralleled by the daily experience of thousands who are unable to see any relation between what they themselves are doing at the moment and the larger and more lasting movements in the opinion and social organization of mankind. He only can be a philosopher who, whatever his school, can view himself and his surroundings, as Spinoza's phrase has it, *sub specie aeternitatis*." *

It is a wonderful experience and wonderful awakening, it changes all life, when first we begin to realize that in our daily life, here and now, we exercise sovereignty,

---

* Annual Report of the President of Columbia University, 1923.

that we can and must choose between right and wrong, that we are in duty bound to assist right and resist evil, that we partake of the divine attribute of personality, and do have our life in the Eternal God. Not in distant lands, or ancient times, not in sacred books or in church councils, not in a new Jerusalem or a heavenly city, not in a future world, but for us here and now all the glory and love of God exist and they constantly uphold us. Each moment partakes of the nature of all eternity, and is equally solemn and equally sacred. To the religious man or woman, every human life is or may become an incarnation of God. One's own duty is to help other lives to become revelations of divine qualities by awakening in them such aspirations through daily exemplification of divine strength and justice and love.

The religious man views all things in God.

"If I ascend up into heaven, Thou art there: if I make my bed in hell, behold Thou art there.

If I take the wings of the morning, and dwell in the uttermost parts of the sea,

Even there shall Thy hand lead me, and Thy right hand shall hold me.

If I say, Surely the darkness shall cover me; even the night shall be light about me.

Yea, the darkness hideth not from Thee; but the night shineth as the day; the darkness and the light are both alike to Thee."*

Theology should relate all spheres of our human earthly life to the eternal truths and abiding realities of the universe. Religion alone gives meaning to daily life and

---

* Psa. 139.

lifts it out of the realm of the commonplace and invests it with divine glory. Needless to say, by religion we mean not outward forms or ceremonies but the life of God in the soul.

The truth and the reality of the affirmative theology stated in this book may be seen by comparing the foregoing conclusions from what may be called its creed with the results of an orthodox creed.

Orthodoxy, as for example set forth in the Apostles' Creed, expresses belief in God the Father Almighty, Maker of heaven and earth, and in Jesus Christ His only Son Our Lord, who was conceived by the Holy Ghost, born of the Virgin Mary, suffered under Pontius Pilate, was crucified, dead and buried, rose again from the dead and ascended to the right hand of God, whence He shall come to judge the quick and the dead. It further recites belief in the Holy Catholic Church, the communion of saints, the forgiveness of sins, the resurrection of the body and the life everlasting.

Apologetics, as the defensive branch of theology, under this belief centers its thought and effort upon the relating of the divine revelation and the divine life, as well as forgiveness of sins and the life everlasting, only to the person and work of Jesus.

Yet the question that is really worth while, that we all, that the whole world, wants to know, is whether we can believe in God the Father Almighty, and what it is so to believe.

In fact, Christianity is more interested in asserting or defending its own particular beliefs, not simply as against those who do not believe in God, in man, and in freedom, and in the glory and divinity of reality, but also and perhaps even more against those who do, than in teaching concerning God the Father Almighty. This is why Christian theology and the Christian creeds seem so remote and even so provincial. The real alternatives are not between Christians and non-Christians, but between idealism and materialism, between belief in God, and either agnosticism or atheism.

We all want to know what personality is, whether it is transient, and to give way to automatism, or whether it is the divine in the human. We want to know what motives ought to govern our actions, whether there are sanctions for sovereignty, divine or human, and how sinful man can be right with God and fit his own life in with God's purposes and how he himself should act toward his sinful fellow-men.

Some have said that sin is the following of outgrown tendencies. In any event the larger and the greater our vision of God, the more do we feel our own weaknesss and the need of constant divine love upon which to lean and in which to trust, so that we may ever follow onward and upward, not apart from the varied relationships of life, but therein to exemplify divine qualities and ourselves share in the divine at-one-ment toward all with whom we come in contact. This means to make belief in goodness, in truth and in loving kindness, in justice and in mercy, easy rather than hard.

It may be that some will read this little book who greatly differ from the writer and believe that he and it are false and heretical. The writer is not concerned with the opinions of any except such as are supremely interested in the truth. If the reader wants to know what is safe or politic, or commonly held or good form, or will be acceptable to bishops or to church councils, his approval is of no value, neither is his condemnation of this book to be regretted. The way to truth is the way of an open mind. With those who follow along that way, the writer is at one regardless of whether present opinions and beliefs are in agreement or as widely at variance as it is possible for them to be.

Not through contentious discussion or partisan debate is the truth to be found, but by careful, patient and honest weighing of evidence. Criticism in the spirit of the love of truth is invited and will be appreciated. No brief is held for fixed or specific opinions. I have believed, therefore have I written, and I am ready to give to myself or to another a reason for the belief now held, but hope never to have a mind closed to new truth or to a larger view of reality. None of us ought to be satisfied with hearsay or with anything less than reality.

The purpose of this *Introduction to Theology* has been to present definitely for consideration certain premises that seem to have been pretty generally neglected. It is hoped and expected, perhaps not soon but ultimately, that a broader and better theology, than that now current and more adequate to meet all human needs, will be developed to be as a guiding star to the lives of nations and of men. The writer has tried simply and clearly to present what seem to him to be important elements to be considered in the development of a body of theological belief and science. The ultimate test of a theology is whether it squares with reality and meets human needs, which are never far from the divine care.

This we do know that no object is more worthy of thoughtful study and deep searching than theology.

Truer insight into the greatest things inevitably will affect all human life. In the words of *The Christian Register*, *"The greatest need of religion is theology."* *

---

* Editorial in issue of December 27, 1923.

THE END

Printed in the United Kingdom
by Lightning Source UK Ltd.
121693UK00001B/75/A